31.25

FEMALE FELONS

FEMALE FELONS

WOMEN AND SERIOUS CRIME
IN
COLONIAL MASSACHUSETTS

N. E. H. HULL

UNIVERSITY OF ILLINOIS PRESS

Urbana and Chicago

This book is printed on acid-free paper.

Library of Congress Cataloging-in-Publication Data

Hull, N. E. H., 1949–
Female felons.

Bibliography: p.
Includes index.
1. Criminal justice, Administration of—Massachusetts
—History.   2. Women offenders—Massachusetts—History.
I. Title.
KFM2478.H85   1987   345.744′03 85-28923
    ISBN 0-252-01315-8 (alk. paper)   347.44053

For Peter,
from his grateful Galatea

CONTENTS

ACKNOWLEDGMENTS

This study would not have been possible without the help, support, and encouragement of the staffs of numerous archives and libraries, teachers, colleagues, and family members. I particularly want to thank the staff of the Supreme Judicial Court, New Suffolk County Courthouse, Boston, the law library of the State Capitol, Boston, the Columbia University Law School Library, the University of Georgia Law School Library, and the Langdell Library of the Harvard Law School. I also want to acknowledge the assistance of the staff of the Harvard Map Collection, Pusey Library, in researching the map.

I am grateful to my teachers who worked with me on various stages of the manuscript as it progressed from seminar papers: Walter Metzger, Richard B. Morris, Rosalind Rosenberg, David Rothman, the late Joseph H. Smith, and most of all my patient and devoted adviser, Alden T. Vaughan. I owe my training in historical quantification to the noble efforts of Richard Jensen, Jan Webster, Daniel Scott Smith, D'Ann Campbell, and the staff of the Newberry Library Summer Institute in Quantitative History and Demography. Finally, I recall with gratitude the late Robert Martinson, who voluntarily took on a student from another university for no compensation and generously imparted his knowledge in the field of sociology and criminal justice.

Several colleagues graciously read and commented on parts of the manuscript at several stages of the writing. All of their criticisms were useful. Bradley Chapin, a dear friend and my undergraduate adviser who was the first to urge me to enter the field of legal history, and Laurel Thatcher Ulrich carefully read and commented on the complete manuscript. Peter Charles Hoffer, my collaborator on other works, tirelessly read and helped edit several versions of the manuscript. I am also grateful to the sponsors and commentators of the Berkshire Conference in Women's History, the Social Science History Association, and the University of Georgia Seminar in Women's History where I presented early versions of three chapters. D. Kelly Weisberg edited and included an earlier version of chapter six in volume one of her collection, *Women and the Law: The Social Historical Perspective,* published by Schenkman Publishing Company. My colleagues in the political science department of the University of Georgia, during the 1979–80 academic year, particularly Loren Beth, Leif Carter, Susette Talarico, and Frank Thompson, provided me with the political scientists' perspective on criminal justice during our many conversations. My equally stimulating colleagues at Vanderbilt University during the spring of 1981, most notably Douglas Leach, Barbara Weinstein, Susan Wiltshire, and Elizabeth Langland, shared their views on history and women's studies with me.

At a critical stage of the preparation of the final version of the manuscript, I received essential financial and moral support from the University of Georgia School of Law. I am deeply grateful to Dean J. Ralph Beaird and Associate Dean Ellen Jordan.

I am also grateful to Richard L. Wentworth and Susan L. Patterson at the University of Illinois Press for their labors in preparing this manuscript for publication.

I want to thank my parents, William and Irene Hull, my father from whom I inherited my love of history and my mother who was always ready to pitch in with the drudgery of sorting cases and who had faith in my ability to accomplish anything I chose to do. Most of all, I want to thank my spouse, whose support for my work never wavered. When I disappeared for months to do research and moved out to write the first draft, our home miraculously continued to run smoothly.

INTRODUCTION

Violent women, conniving women, immoral women, women "without the sight of Gd before their eyes"; desperate women, who drove judges and ministers not easily shocked into bewildered fury; penitent women, weary women, brutal women, and innocent women; women accused, indicted, tried, convicted, and punished for crimes laid to their charge; women displayed to their neighbors and friends as veritable Bathshebas; and women allowed to "go without delay" back to their homes and families: these are the subjects of this book. So, too, are the men who shared this uncertain, mobile, violent world: legislators and ministers, judges and jurors, magistrates and constables, all holding offices closed to women; husbands and lovers, witnesses and victims, anxious to have their say in court; men accused of serious crimes who shared the jailyard and the dock. In authority, these men's perceptions determined the fate of female defendants. The fate of less fortunate men, indicted for serious crimes, allows the scholar to weigh suspicions of gender-based prejudice in the laws and courts.

For its drama and historical value alone, the story of women accused of serious crimes in colonial Massachusetts is surely worth telling, but the tale has a larger significance as well. Although women comprised a small portion of the total number of defendants for felonies and homicides—then, as now, little more than 10 percent—their criminality reveals much about the world in which they lived and how (and why) they failed to cope with it. Crime is never "typical" behavior; it is the dangerous extremity of abnormality that a society will not tolerate. Crime demonstrates the priorities of a society, and the anger and frustration of those left out, or behind, in those priorities.

1

It is hardly necessary to justify the investigation of crime in our own day. We are preoccupied with "crime in the city," "white-collar crime," "computer crime," "organized crime," and "violent crime." Law enforcement is a growth industry, for which academic research into the roots and cures for crime is handmaiden. As legislators and law enforcement officials have focused upon the minority-group suspect and victim, so current criminology has fixed its eye upon homosexuals, blacks, Hispanics, and, not the least, women. Unfortunately, a generation of research has produced only controversy about the causes and cures of women's criminality. Apparently women are at once paternally protected, systematically abused, forgiven their trespasses, and made scapegoats for men's problems. And all this in an era that claims (with some justice) to be a new day for women.

One way to put this controversy over the putative sexism of America's criminal justice system into perspective is to set modern findings into their historical context. Women have been prosecuted for serious crimes in this country for over three hundred years. We need to know whether women committed different sorts of crimes at different rates from men, and how the handling of their crimes differed from the treatment of men's. We must have genuine historical depth, a real comparison, not something along the lines of "pre-1950" compared to "post-1950." Only after true historical comparisons— studies of changes over long periods of time—can we assess the impact of sexual prejudice upon the definition of criminal behavior and the prosecution of crime among women.

In the past two decades, historians, motivated by many of the same impulses as criminologists, have turned their attention to minorities. We have seen, in sequence, the rise of black history, ethnic history, and women's history. The last of these has proven a durable and voluminous field, exploring the internal lives of ordinary women as well as the way in which a male-dominated legal and political system structured those lives. At the intersection of modern concerns about deviant women and historical research lies the wealth of evidence stored in historical archives. One such archive, indeed the most complete, reliable, and sustained record of criminal activity and law enforcement within a single early American jurisdiction, contains the criminal records of the supreme judicial courts of colonial Massachusetts. Authorities in the Bay Colony were meticulous recordkeepers. They believed signs of divine will were everywhere present, and no sign was to be overlooked. Compared to the records of English assize court officials (some of whom were also Puritans), the Massachusetts highest courts records were veritable paragons of neatness. These are the docket books, file papers, and minutes of the General Court, the Court of Assistants, and (after 1691) the Superior Court of Judicature. To these courts came all women and men accused of serious offenses.[1] In case after case, many recorded in great detail, over a century and a half, justice was meted out—enough cases to compute rates of crime and to compare the treatment of men and women over time. Here is an opportunity to give historical context to the mass of modern studies, to seek the roots of modern attitudes, and even, at certain points, to assess the success and failure of alternative methods to ours.

But this study is not wholly present-minded; no historian ought to forget that her primary materials—the records of crime, the statutes and common laws, the evidences of attitude—were rooted in a world that no longer exists. Unlike our own bustling, postindustrial society, Puritan Massachusetts was a society poised between almost medieval religious rigor and a more modern materialistic vigor. Within its confines were those who sought a sanctuary from corruption and those who pursued profit and luxury. If the great mass of its denizens were ordinary working people, servants and serving maids, agricultural day laborers, cartmen, craftsmen and their apprentices, shipwrights and their assistants, and a steadily growing number of marginally employed sailors, "mechanicks," and former soldiers, the tone of its society was set by its spiritual founders. Nevertheless, as time passed, life in its towns, originally organized around its licensed churches, grew more modern in the first century of settlement. Outsiders, warned off when they arrived, could not be put off forever. Young people, unable to obtain land within the original boundaries of their parents' grants, "hived out" to new towns in the west or made their way to Boston. Now a center of trade, commerce, banking, and light manufacturing, the capital experienced waves of expansion and depression, war, disease, and overcrowding—all ripening conditions for crime.

The role played by women in this society mixed the traditional and the novel. Theirs was a special place, not altogether enviable—for in this land of saints and sinners, they were viewed as both saintlier and more sinful than men. The contradiction, really a duality, appeared in sermons and admonitory literature. The Puritan woman was a docile helpmeet— daughter and wife were vessels of grace capable of election to heaven, but aggressive pursuit of this goal, as Anne Hutchinson discovered, led only to grief. While the stereotype of the meek Puritan woman lived on in the literature, Massachusetts women did not conform to its outlines. Puritan wives and non-Puritan maids, Indian women, black women, Scots and Irish women, Huguenot women, and Dutch women, *femes sole,* and independent-minded daughters of the well-to-do lived in great variety of circumstances. Indeed, the vast majority of women in Massachusetts were not orthodox Puritans at all. Even among those who were, quite a few managed the family business or farm, dealt with debtors and creditors, and engaged in certain forms of public activity. No woman could vote, hold office, or serve in the militia or on a jury, limitations that influenced their fate as criminal defendants in subtle ways, but neither were they the women of Periclean Athens, ordered to the private sphere and kept there. When they violated the norms imposed upon them, they became the objects of scorn and dire warning: lessons for others in the havoc of the Fall.

Sin and the Fall—the self-humbling language of Reformation Protestantism—rang in the courts and churches of New England, just as in the mother country. The diction of indictment and sentencing linked lawlessness to damnation. Were women the special targets of this condemnatory rhetoric? The same pronouncement of divine censure fell upon male as on female defendants, but modern scholars dispute the substance beneath the surface of Puritan criminal laws and courts. Some have discerned in the very marrow of Puritan piety a core of sexism; others have found a mild and generally fair-minded

4

magistracy. For some historians the prejudice against deviant women extended to all women; for others, the networks of mutual support and caring that women built are far more important. From lower court records, there is evidence of both impartiality and partiality on the basis of gender. Certainly, as the following chapters will demonstrate, there was potential for discrimination against women on a wide scale, but was that prospect realized? Was it linked to Puritanism itself or to other forces? Did it abate with the coming of the age of the American Revolution?

Using a variety of methods drawn from criminology, comparative criminal law, and quantitative analysis, I have tried to explore the relationship between potential and actual prejudice. The two tests I have used throughout the book are ones that must be administered, whatever the initial (or final) position one takes in the historiographical debate. First, how does the handling of women compare to the handling of men in the law and in the courts? Second, how are given defendants of both sexes treated over time, in particular from the heyday of Puritanism to its abatement on the eve of the Revolution?

The order of the chapters herein moves from the general to the specific: to wit, from notions of deviance and the broad development of the criminal law toward the punishment of individual offenders. The idea of crime rests upon variable conceptions of wrongful conduct. The state makes certain wrongs liable to punishment because these pose intolerable threats to public morals, property, and personal safety. Just who defines these boundaries is a subject of controversy among modern scholars; in Chapter 1, I will explore the fashioners of New England Puritan ideas of right and wrong and how these ideas were applied to women. Criminal codes, additional statutes on crime, and customary or common understandings of criminal behavior changed greatly even during the Puritans' tenure as New England's lawgivers. Most striking among these changes were "women's crimes." The rise (and fall) of the wanton woman in the penal laws is the subject of Chapter 2. The law defines criminality in Anglo-American jurisdictions: there is no crime without a law. In the era we study, the organs of government that made the laws—the assembly (when it sat in the General Court with the Assistants) and the upper houses—were also courts. The Court of Assistants was also the supreme court and the senate of Massachusetts until 1686; its bench heard cases under the laws that it passed. In chapters 3–5, I explore the connection between potential gender bias in the laws and actual bias in the criminal justice system. Chapter 3 displays the extent of serious women's crimes and compares them to men's. Chapter 4 traces the treatment of women from reports of their offenses through their pleading at trial. Chapter 5 follows their trials. The mirror of crime in this era was held by the men responsible for ferreting out and punishing crime, that is, the criminal record is the court record. With few exceptions, we have lost the evidence of crime that preceded official inquiry into it. Thus, if there is a bias against women in the system, it will protrude into the pattern of crime.

If putative biases in the labeling of criminals cannot be separated from the simple fact of arrest or prosecution, they can be teased from the record by isolating and measuring the forces generated by the system itself—shifts in priorities among the magistrates, new attitudes among jurors, and changes in the pattern of law enforcement. In effect, we try to see into the record, by giving it depth. Historians do not have the luxury of firsthand observation, interviews with jurors, witnesses, and victims, and day-to-day coverage of trials, but we do have the advantage of time, of viewing the accumulation of shifts in attitude, discretion, and outcome over decades and centuries. The last two chapters make most forthright use of this perspective. Chapter 6 explains the mechanism behind punishment in the high courts of colonial Massachusetts and traces a significant change in these over time. Chapter 7 reaches from the colonies to the present, to place the changing rates of homicide in modern America into their proper historical perspective, an example of what historians can do for modern criminology and policy planners.

NOTE

1. The General Court—the deputies (lower house) and assistants (upper house) meeting as a court of first instance, appeal, or equity—had progressively less criminal business brought before it from 1634 to 1686. It

heard only two criminal cases between 1680 and 1686 and lost all of its criminal jurisdiction during the Dominion of New England and second charter periods, after 1686. On the earlier period, see Barbara A. Black, "The Judicial Power and the General Court in Early Massachusetts" (Ph.D. diss., Yale University, 1975), 169–89.

CHAPTER ONE

WOMEN AND DEVIANCE

Deviance is nonconforming behavior, but not all nonconforming behavior leads to social or civil sanctions. Circumstances—formal law, norms, or even family styles—determine how far any individual may stray with impunity from conventionality. Deviance is normal in the sense that every society, no matter how small or homogeneous, has within it those who test its rules or push beyond its boundaries.[1] Indeed, some individuals may be labeled as deviants without engaging in proscribed behavior. They are simply seen as likely candidates for such behavior—"the usual suspects." Such anticipatory deviance may occur in a church, finding sinners within its own congregants; a family, fashioning its own "black sheep"; or within a state, seeking corrupters of its youth, subjurators of its policies, or spies for its enemies.[2] Deviance functions in a social setting to reinforce group mores—consensus on the wrongfulness of the deviant's conduct. The trial and punishment or exile or shaming of the deviant may physically bring a community together.[3] For this reason, in times of particular stress communities pay disproportionate attention to deviants and suspected deviants within their midst. These are times for soul-searching, in which devils lurking within are discerned and decried in "different" others. These are the occasions of witch hunts, real and figurative.

In a book on women's crimes written from the perspective of modern scholarship, it is easy to be myopic on the subject of deviance. Whatever our views on the liberation of women today, we must recognize that early American society was no more concerned with sexual discrimination than with racial discrimination. Women occupied a subordinate position in society, an inferiority nowhere better demonstrated than in the Anglo-American common law. While the unmarried adult

9

woman—the *feme sole*—had most of the common law rights over property, the married woman had little right to her own property. Her husband had a life interest in her estate, to use, or lose, as he wished. Courts in early America did guard the dower rights of the widow and allowed premarital property divisions, protecting the possessions of a woman from her husband's heirs far more assiduously than in England, but the children, not the widow, received the bulk of intestate estates.[4] Women had very limited power to make contracts, bring suits, or contest wills. In the public sphere women could not hold office, vote, serve on juries (except "matron's juries" to determine whether a criminal defendant was pregnant), or act as legal counsel. These restrictions applied to all women, married, widowed, and single.

The explanation for these legal detriments was simple: women were the weaker sex—too weak to protect their property against seizure. The common law did not openly adopt this rationale, but it was assumed everywhere in the civil and criminal courts. As a recent commentator on the medieval property laws has written: "The preference of males to females [in the order of inheritance of real property] hardly needs explanation; obviously the rule is natural where land is held by knight-service."[5] Where might of arms determined legality, women might naturally suffer an inferior status. Of course, in disputed cases the courts might have taken the view that such imposed debilities required extra efforts at protection (as modern courts have developed the doctrine of equal protection of the laws), but the view taken by early English courts was just as logical: women had to be protected by men, in whose legal capacity the daughter's or wife's property would be safe. Such laws were the accumulation of five hundred years of Anglo-Norman jurisprudence. They combined a sympathy for women's supposed incapacity with compensating debility. A few examples of this reasoning will suffice, for they are typical of all. Women were not liable to trial by ordeal; the church would not permit it, and chivalric notions dismissed it. To compensate for this immunity from challenge, they were permitted to bring only two actions against others in the king's court: charges of rape, and wrongful death of their husbands. Other appeals of felony had to be brought by men, who could face a trial of their accusations by combat.[6] In later years, women could not be prosecuted for certain crimes that they committed at the behest of their husbands, for women's personalities were legally merged with their husbands. They were *femes covert.* In return for this protection, they lost the power to participate fully in the system that condemned their husbands and other men to corporal and capital punishments.

These and other laws rested upon the assumption of women's inferiority. In a society where status came from bearing arms, women were at a disadvantage. Though as daughters and wives of powerful men, women did influence the course of medieval history, their power of direct action was blocked by the very chivalry that purported to defend their honor. At the same time they were not the special target of the laws: laws on property and appeal of felony were not designed to abuse women. The rise of Puritanism in England ushered in a different and more dangerous role for women in society. Puritan influence made women's place more defined and their deviance more pronounced. Upright, they were the vessels of sweetest grace; fallen, they became the tools of Satan himself.

Puritanism, the reform movement of a second generation of English Calvinists, decried all remnants of Catholicism in English liturgy, church organization, and canon law. Often well educated and well connected, Puritan ministers and the children of their fellowship, the congregations that they led, were outspoken and indefatigable in their efforts to direct English life.[7] Unlike their medieval predecessors, who understood passion as well as abstinence, most Puritan thinkers were utterly opposed to the display of sexuality by women. Righteous women were demure; pious women were not objects of passion. To be sure, the Puritan did not want ascetic saints as helpmeets; this was a perversion upon God's laws fostered by the Roman church. Instead, Puritan ministers extolled the modest, obedient, hard-working daughter, wife, and mother. No idealizations for them (either of saints or of courtly lovers), women were created to help men work toward their sanctification. The core of this presumably realistic approach to women was an obsession with the danger of female sexuality. Closely controlled by husbands and fathers and checked by the women themselves, female sexual activity was acceptable. Left

11

to its own rules, it was a garden grown wild. And men's souls could be lost in it forever. The seductive female was the devil's finest tool.[8] It is not difficult to demonstrate the transmission of these attitudes from Old to New England. Themes of female weakness and dependence abounded in New England ministers' sermons.[9] Such normative stipulations penetrated the home and the marketplace in the early years of settlement. "Un-womanly women," too assertive, too blatant in their feelings or too ardent in their passions, were silenced or exiled. While overt piety remained praiseworthy, attempts to adopt male roles of preaching or pursuing the opposite sex were censured. Anne Hutchinson, who dared to call ministers and magistrates ungodly, was the best known of those who suffered for their independence of mind, but other women—recalcitrant Quakers, uppity servants, and resentful slaves—were also singled out for punishment.[10]

Men who questioned the established clergy, flaunted their Quakerism, or disobeyed their masters were punished as severely as women, and, indeed, the preponderance of these acts were committed by men (a fact too easily ignored). Nevertheless, men's serious crimes were not characterized or feared as evidence of God's displeasure with this new Zion in the same way as women's crimes were. Men were obstinate and disorderly by nature; when women behaved in the same fashion, they violated the roles magistrates and ministers assigned to "good wives." This process of labeling transformed the female suspect into a symbol of deviance far more visible and striking than her male counterpart. When women disobeyed, the devil was abroad, for, as Cotton Mather and other ministers told the judges, the devil worked through women. Male crimes—indeed, at a rate far larger than we have today—were not a sign of impending doom. Females, already under special scrutiny for their potential corruptiveness, committed the same crimes as men with very different effect upon their neighbors and their rulers.

Reinforcement of normative standards—the acceptance of others' prescription for one's behavior—was both negative and positive in seventeenth-century New England. The goodwife was praised and thought highly of in her town. Whether rich or poor, she was greeted at church and in the lane. Motherhood and good stewardship of family holdings were valued. For the erring or fallen woman there was shame: excommunication from church or sentence to the ducking stool (for being a scold) or to the pillory (for slander or fornication). When the offender curbed her ways, positive reinforcements reappeared. Churches allowed the repentant to return, and authorities made allowances for good behavior. A system as complete as this should have worked to dampen misconduct by women, but it did not. Not only did women persist in calling each other, and men, foul names, threatening each other with bodily harm, and raising a ruckus, but also they specialized in the very behaviors that magistrates and ministers feared. They fornicated, in increasing numbers and at accelerating rates, throughout the century. Some women simply did not internalize the norms laid down for them by men.

While some women were repeat offenders, most lost their heads or their hearts but once or twice and ended up in court.[11] These women were not regarded as monsters and received the same punishments as men convicted of similar crimes. Thus the records remind us that the ideal Puritan woman was a creation of men's minds, much as today men fantasize about ideal mates. The reality of attitude as well as behavior was quite different. When one turns from Cotton Mather and a few other conservative divines, to less well-known preachers and recorders of everyday life, one finds a much more realistic picture of women. They were valued for their individual traits and human qualities, rather than for their embodiment of abstract religious virtues.[12] Of course, they had to be aware of death; the frailty of life surrounded them in their infants' diseases and their own postpartum weakness. Nevertheless, some of them outlived husbands and sons, inherited property, ran farms and shops, and directed male servants, laborers, and craftsmen. If some men saw them as weak, others recognized their strength, for to survive and prosper in that age a woman had to be strong.

The single greatest challenge to this pattern in the seventeenth century was the witchcraft trials held in Salem during 1692 and 1693. Women predominated among the accused, as they always did among these prosecutions in New England. Of the 103 persons implicated in witchcraft before the Salem episode, 83 were women.[13] Men could be warlocks, but the mechanics of identifying witches and the structural nature of the crimes pointed to female perpetrators. Mostly older women, living on the outskirts of town off the charity of their neighbors, they were not a respected group. Their neighbors and the magistrates truly believed that witches were in league with the devil and through his power could harm others. The courts in Old and New England required evidence of this harm before indicting a suspect (merely covenanting with the devil was not an offense in the civil courts, as it was in France and Germany). The Salem witchcraft indictments were remarkable, not only for their sex distribution, but also for their outcome. Never before had so many been found guilty, upon such skimpy evidence.[14]

The women tried at Salem faced a virulent antifeminine hysteria whose root was not misogyny per se but a complex case of religious anxiety. When the special courts convened in the town, the judges sought the advice of the ministers on the admissibility of spectral evidence (evidence invisible to the jurors). The ministerial fellowship, led by Cotton Mather, avowed their belief in the invisible kingdom of the devil, and the trials proceeded rapidly. The bench had never before sought the advice of ministers on matters of criminal law, nor did it ever again. This was the first of a number of aberrations in the conduct of these trials, which were motivated by concern for the survival of the Puritan faith, not the chastisement of women. Women who confessed to practicing witchcraft, a felony punishable by death, were pardoned—another anomaly, for confession of murder, piracy, or treason did not lead to pardon. Finally, after a year of trials and executions, the court reversed itself on the admissibility of spectral evidence and released the vast majority of the accused. Throughout the episode husbands stood by their accused wives, even at the risk of bringing accusations upon themselves. The courage of some of the accused women brought tears to the eyes of those who had gathered to see them hanged, a complete reversal of the effect such scenes were supposed to have. Some of the judges and ministers in charge of the trials, looking back upon the events in which they had played a part, renounced their roles and prayed to God for forgiveness.

Were we to leap ahead to the era of the American Revolution, we would find a different situation: "The decade of turbulence that preceded the Revolution touched the lives of women as well as men."[15] Women were politicized. In Massachusetts patriotic women extended their roles to include management of community concerns, clubs and societies, and even their own informal committees of correspondence. A few women even ventured to lecture men on the proper conduct of politics and to suggest that women play some role in it. While Abigail Adams's instructions to her husband to "remember the ladies" in the new continental government were atypical (as atypical as she was of her gender), the coming crisis raised real hopes as well as fears for the future.[16] As dramatic as this change in role might appear, it must be qualified, for the vast majority of women were not intimately involved in the politics of upheaval. The sphere of activity of ordinary women grew less dramatically. Gradually, over the course of a century, educational and vocational opportunities would allow them some control over their children and their property.[17]

More important, even for the Abigails, a larger role in public life and a freer hand in the private sphere required preparation. One would expect that the two great intellectual reforms of the era would have lifted women from their lowly place toward equality with men. The Great Awakening and the Enlightenment did nothing of the kind. It is true that young women were among the targets of the leading Great Awakening preachers. Jonathan Edwards, for example, from his Northampton pulpit, gloried in the conversion of several young women. Other ministers recorded similar triumphs, but these were achievements precisely because of the inherent frailty of women.[18] Overall, the struggle for control of church government between Old and New Lights, each claiming to be holier than the other, did not liberate women, though it did contribute to an increase in their attendance in churches. The Enlightenment, refashioning the ideas of the physical world and human society along more rational, empirically discoverable lines, was concerned little with the question of women's place. With the exception of the magnificent matrons of a handful of Paris salons and a few notable English writers and thinkers, women played little part in the scientific revolutions that swept from Europe through America in the early part of the eighteenth century.[19] While a few enlightened thinkers (notably Benjamin Franklin) held advanced views on women, the subject was far less interesting to the philosophers than it had been to the Puritans.

The key to the rising status of women was not in formal intellectual movements, where women were not engaged, but in the most characteristic women's activity of all: mothering. In England and in New England, changing attitudes toward parenthood followed changes in the lives of well-to-do families in the eighteenth century. Whether through an improvement in the standard of living or from some deeper wellspring of human emotion, the rearing of children was altered. Perhaps the forces that had disrupted the social harmony of the early modern village and had led to the campaign against witchcraft and infanticide were forming a new pattern of social convention. Nuclear families were not novel, but the attention lavished upon the children in their midst was unlike that of earlier generations. Mortality rates of children had begun to decline. Wet nursing was going out of fashion. Infant medical care discontinued swaddling, purges, confining harnesses, and other restrictive measures. Evidence from diaries and letters also suggests that families were closer and more affectionate in the post-1700 era than they had been in earlier generations.[20]

The new social valuation of the child encouraged mothers to give more attention to infants. In this respect, the middle and upper classes provided a model. J. H. Plumb has concluded that "from what we do know, there can be no doubt that the children's world of the 18th century—at least for those born higher up the social scale than the laboring poor—changed dramatically." Expenditures for schools, the appearance of children's books written for the children, and fashions and toys for the young market all showed increasing adult concern for the pleasure of children. New England colonial parents were constantly being warned by magistrates and clergymen against the excesses of doting affection for their children, a certain evidence that such excesses were growing. It can be presumed that something of this emotional and material expenditure probably seeped down to the less-fortunate parents of children.[21]

The new views of motherhood in particular and the growth of romantic sentimentality in general almost surely had a potent effect upon the attitudes of men in positions of authority. In matters of sexual morality, that signal of women's guilt for earlier generations of judges and juries, courts were becoming less severe. Although officials in Old and New England continued to rail at incontinence, the weakened control that parents had over their older children undermined the officials' power to enforce sexual regularity. By the late eighteenth century in New England, "the experience of law enforcement in America as well as intellectual influences combined to suggest practical limits to what the law could accomplish in enforcement of morals."[22]

Women had always been mothers. But as the role of mothering was raised to new importance in the society, men reassessed the importance of women and found a new sympathy for their sufferings. These new attitudes radiated simultaneously into polite literature and into rough-and-tumble street life. Even criminal law, often a generation or two behind shifts in attitudes, slowly bent to the new valuation of women. The Puritan age had passed, not with a bang, but with the whimper of infants in arms.

NOTES

1. Marshall B. Clinard and Robert F. Meier, *Sociology of Deviant Behavior*, 5th ed. (New York, 1979), 12–23.

2. Stuart H. Traub and Craig B. Little, eds., *Theories of Deviance* (Itasca, Ill., 1975), 159–62.

3. Emile Durkheim, *The Rules of Sociological Method*, trans. S. A. Solvaay and G. H. Mueller (New York, 1958), 67.

4. Richard B. Morris, *Studies in the History of American Law*, 2d ed. (New York, 1958), 126–200. New England was for its time an enlightened jurisdiction in these questions, conceding to women rights to property and standing to sue. In the area of divorce, for example, the Court of Assistants did allow petitions for divorce from women for a variety of causes, a civil process far more liberal, in theory, than the church courts allowed in England. See D. Kelly Weisberg, "Under Great Temptations Here: Women and Divorce Law in Puritan Massachusetts," *Feminist Studies* 2 (1975), 183–94. For conditions in the South, where customs were different, see Marylynn Salmon, "Women and Property in South Carolina: The Evidence from Marriage Settlements, 1730–1830," *William and Mary Quarterly*, 3d ser., 39 (1982), 656 *n30*.

5. A. W. B. Simpson, *An Introduction to the History of the Land Law* (Oxford, 1961), 55.

6. Ruth Kittel, "Rape in Thirteenth-Century England: A Study of the Common-Law Courts," in D. Kelly Weisberg, ed., *Women and the Law: A Social Historical Perspective* (Cambridge, Mass., 1982), 2:101–16.

7. Patrick Collinson, *The Elizabethan Puritan Movement* (Berkeley, 1967), 57.

8. Katharine M. Rodgers, *The Troublesome Helpmate: A History of Misogyny in Literature* (Seattle, 1966), 135–59, and see pp. 10–11 above.

9. Laurel Thatcher Ulrich, *Good Wives: Image and Reality in the Lives of Women in Northern New England* (New York, 1982).

10. Lyle Koehler, *A Search for Power: The "Weaker Sex" in Seventeenth-Century New England* (Urbana, Ill., 1980), 28–61, 189–263.

11. See pp. 56–57 below.

12. Laurel Thatcher Ulrich, "Virtuous Women Found: New England Ministerial Literature, 1668–1735," *American Quarterly* 28 (Spring 1976), 40: "Most housewives in provincial Boston were probably too occupied with the daily round to consider the nature of their position in society."

13. Koehler, *Search for Power*, 474–80. The calculations are my own.

14. For further details, see pp. 49–50.

15. Mary Beth Norton, *Liberty's Daughters: The Revolutionary Experience of American Women* (Boston, 1980), 155.

16. Charles W. Akers, *Abigail Adams: An American Woman* (Boston, 1980), 31–47.

17. See, for example, Frank Stricker, "Cookbooks and Lawbooks: The Hidden History of Career Women in Twentieth-Century America," *Journal of Social History* 10 (Fall 1976), 1–19.

18. Jonathan Edwards, "Narrative of Surprising Conversions" (May 30, 1735), in *Jonathan Edwards: Representative Selections*, ed. Clarence H. Faust and Thomas H. Johnson, rev. ed. (New York, 1962), 79–80.

19. Linda K. Kerber, *Women of the Republic: Intellect and Ideology in Revolutionary America* (Chapel Hill, N.C., 1980), 13–32.

20. Lawrence Stone, *The Family, Sex, and Marriage in England, 1500–1800* (New York, 1977), especially 449–78, places the watershed of the affective nuclear domestic group's modernity at 1640. Thereafter, generations of children, themselves becoming parents, began to express warmth and affection for children more freely. Alice Ryerson, "Medical Advice on Childrearing, 1550–1900," *Harvard Educational Review* 41 (1961), finds 1750 the turning point in improvement of infant-care advice.

21. J. H. Plumb, "The New World of Children in Eighteenth-Century England," *Past and Present* 67 (May 1975), 65; Ross W. Beales, "In Search of the Historical Child: Miniature Adulthood and Youth in Colonial New England," *American Quarterly* 27 (Oct. 1975), 396.

22. David H. Flaherty, "Law and the Enforcement of Morals in Early America," *Perspectives in American History* 5 (1971), 250–51.

CHAPTER TWO

WOMEN AND THE FELONY LAW

The Puritan view of women as potential receptacles of immorality crept into the felony law in both Old and New England. As Roscoe Pound once admitted, the law is often the tool of dominant groups, and the Puritan ministry had the ear, if not the rod, of the Puritan magistry.[1] These lawgivers' and law enforcers' religious aims could have produced a pervasive bias in the criminal law.

It can be argued that criminal laws, particularly laws against heinous crimes, do not regard the status, wealth, or sex of the accused and the victim, but express the shared anger and repugnance of an entire society. Viewed from the perspective of the lawgiver (that is, using only the materials he leaves behind), this conclusion can be easily maintained. The suspects' views of the law are discarded, in effect prejudging the issue in every case in favor of the prosecution. Traditional arguments of this sort find no credence in modern scholarship. Historians now recognize that criminal law is a form of social control as well as an expression of deep-seated moral aversions. While acts "evil in themselves"—*mala in se* crimes such as murder, burglary, and arson—are prohibited in almost every Western criminal code, the great bulk of criminal law concerns offenses *mala prohibita*, which are evil because, at a particular time and place, statute proscribed them.[2] Certain sexual behavior and public demonstrations allowed in one society, for example, homophilic lovemaking in private and dancing in public markets, were performed without censure in Hellenic Athens but were punished in Puritan Massachusetts.[3] Laws against such acts not only prohibit behavior, but they also label classes of potential offenders. Laws against prostitution, for example, may require proof that a proposition of the illicit activity was made, but women in scanty attire in disrepu-

19

table districts are often assumed to be soliciting customers. If local authorities set out to curb this traffic, they label such women as likely offenders and arrest them without proof of an explicit proposition. No system of administration of criminal justice based upon *mala prohibita* can be neutral in its view of potential criminals. For this reason, moreover, *mala prohibita* crimes function as social control mechanisms, regulating the conduct of certain "dangerous classes." Criminal law invariably falls more heavily upon classes, sects, and ethnic groups at the fringes of society, whose behavior threatens dominant values and power structures. These concerns, entirely unrelated to provable culpability in particular cases, can have great impact upon the framing of criminal law.[4]

The framing of criminal law is a social process and so reflects the fears and desires of community leaders, some of which are widely shared in the community, others of which reflect a struggle to maintain power and control behavior. As the social values of lawmakers and judges—the formal givers of statute and precedent—change, so the letter of the law changes. In the courtroom itself the evolution of values among grand and petty jurors will influence how they see and decide upon the facts presented to them. Often the jurors, occasionally with the assent of a judge, will run athwart the letter of the law, making it more lenient or modifying it to fit circumstances not anticipated by the statute-writers. Changes in statute often lag generations behind changes in values, though statute follows—at a distance—practice in the courts. The changing law of crimes mirrors and gives force to changing attitudes toward offenders and offenses in the world outside the courtroom.

To understand the shifting place of women in the felony law, we must also recognize the constraints of gender. Speaking generally, the felony law of England and her American colonies applied to both women and men. But women did not make law: they were not the judges who "discovered" the common law in their courts nor the legislators who wrote statutes. It is true that most men had little part in the making of law in this era, too. The few who could vote for the fewer still who sat in the House of Commons in England represented a very small segment of society. After 1691, no one voted for the judges; before that time, the deputies chose the Assistants. The lower judiciary was appointed. In the colonies many more men could participate in the legislative process than in England, but the poorest and least-established men still could not.

Nevertheless, the absence of women from the lawmaking and law enforcement processes was more profound in its consequences for women than the similar absence of most men was for men. The interests of women as a group were not represented or, if represented, were seen through men's eyes, while the rights and concerns of poor men could at least be heard among their betters' councils. Women's isolation from power was more significant because women were more different from men than poor men were from rich men. Poor men might be defended by those who shared their poverty, but women had no chance of officially voicing their complaints or desires in public meetings. They were a silent and easily victimized majority, or rather became such when their "betters" so decided. And that is just what happened with the rise of Puritanism.

For three centuries, from the first commentaries on the common law to the eve of the ascension of Elizabeth I, the position of women in felony law remained unchanged. The concept of felony, though in its origins still somewhat obscure to scholars, clearly did not have any particular interst in, much less bias against, women. Within four decades after 1558, women in England and New England became very visible subjects of felony law, to their great detriment. Only when the legislators of Massachusetts began to refashion criminal law in the eighteenth century did the concern for crimes associated with women diminish. To trace these changes, one must begin with the concept of felony itself.

While the origin of felony law is obscure, its purpose was evident from its inception. Felony was a class of offenses introduced by the Norman invaders to protect their lives and property from the native Saxons. The word itself may have been derived from the German or Saxon *fee*, for estate, and *lon*, for value.[5] A felony was a crime whose punishment was forfeiture of estates. The forfeiture might be limited to personal chattels or extend to the inheritance of an entire family.[6] In England forfeiture was the punishment for felonies, particularly for treason.[7] If the penalty that initially differentiated felony from other crimes was forfeiture—loss of property and disinheritance—it was a punishment directed at grown men, particularly heads of families. Treasons, crimes committed upon the king's land, and crimes against Normans by Saxons—the first English felonies—infrequently involved women. The felony law did not exempt women, but women were not ordinarily heads of households with property to forfeit and thus were rarely jeopardized by felony law.

A second definition of felony focused upon the crime, rather than the punishment of forfeiture, but it, too, tended to reduce the visibility of female offenders. In his *Institutes* Sir Edward Coke argued that felony originated from the Latin word *fel*, signifying gall, or the Saxon word *fell*, meaning fierce. According to Coke, felonies were crimes committed with a fiercely malicious intent.[8] The felon intended to accomplish great mischief. The law dictionaries of Giles Jacob and Thomas Wood repeated Coke: felonies were crimes with evil intent.[9] As Sir William Blackstone admitted, forfeiture, "corruption of the blood," was no longer the punishment for most felonies, and evil intent, *mens rea*, was a necessary part of the prosecutor's case against a felon.[10] Despite criticism of Coke's etymology by later commentators, the great chief justice nevertheless came closer to the modern meaning of felony. Women were certainly considered capable of fierce crimes and were regularly prosecuted for them. In fourteenth-century England, one of every ten accused felons was female. Using knives and hatchets, their favorite weapons, and less often, poison, women killed husbands, children, and relatives.[11] Nevertheless, throughout early English history, women felons were indicted and tried far less often than men. Only 8.6 percent of all persons accused of murder in thirteenth-century England were women.[12] Fierce crimes were not likely to be linked with women in the minds of jurists and legislators.

Severity of sentence was a third hallmark of felony law. When Michael Dalton and William Hawkins introduced the topic of felony in their seventeenth-century works and Wood defined "felony" a few years later, they all associated it with capital punishment. Hawkins reported that common law capital offenses were felonies by definition.[13] Dalton did distinguish "lesser felonies" not requiring the noose. Many of these were felonies by statute, Parliament disregarding both forfeiture and capital punishment in its own definitions of felony.[14] By the mid-eighteenth century Blackstone argued that felonies were merely crimes whose punishments were severe, rather than a concept or class of offenses.[15]

Women certainly knew the severity of the law and occasionally suffered death for committing felonies. Nevertheless, felony law accorded them special avenues of escape not given to men: pregnancy and *feme covert* status. At Old Salisbury jail on January 30, 1276: "Edith de Halmerton, taken at Henton with Robert [Boket] her husband for stealing sheep at Aulton [Fulton] Priors, for which theft Robert was hanged in Selkele hundred and she being pregnant was sent to Salisbury gaol and there kept until her parturition, says she was Robert's wife. Jury of 12 of Selkele and Swaneborg hundreds sufficiently declare that she his espoused wife." She was acquitted. After a fetus had quickened, that is, had begun to move in the mother's uterus, ecclesiastical law considered the infant alive. Pregnant women convicted of felony could then "plead their belly" and obtain a stay of execution of sentence until three months after delivery. In that time, the defendant might obtain a pardon, get pregnant again (for the jails were not segregated by sex), or even become lost in the machinery of justice. Quickening was determined by the examination of a jury of matrons, one of the few official duties women performed in the criminal justice system. Women thus had the power to save other women from the noose.[16]

Edith owed her stay to pregnancy, but her acquittal was based upon her marital status. A married woman was exempt from prosecution for certain felonies that she committed with her husband, for it was assumed that she was under his direction or orders. *Feme covert* was a civil law concept derived from the property and inheritance law of marriage.[17] Indeed, under the rule of *feme covert*, a woman could not be charged with stealing property from her husband. Coke reported: "The Wife cannot steal the Goods of her husband, for they be not the goods of another; for the husband and wife are one person in law."[18] Out of these principles emerged the doctrine that a wife could not be convicted of a crime her husband forced her to commit, since she could not legally refuse his commands. Coke made the related criminal points: "A *femme covert* committeth not larceny, if it be done by the coertion of her husband; but a *femme covert* may commit Larceny, if she doth it without the coertion of her husband; and there it appeareth, that a man may be accessory to his wife, but the wife cannot be accessory to her husband, though she know that he committed Larceny, and . . . discover it not; for by the law Divine she is not bound to discover the offense of her husband."[19] Wood noted that when the wife joined in the theft, the coercion of her husband was "presum'd."[20] Thus, under *feme covert* women were routinely excused from harsh punishments for some felonies. Murder, treason, and burglary were exempt from this rule, but since women rarely committed such crimes, the exceptions had little bearing on their treatment. Under none of the forfeiture, fierceness, or capital punishment definitions of felony did women occupy an important place in felony law, nor could it be said that felony law had any prejudice against them.

There is a last, more comprehensive definition of felony, subsuming all the others,[21] which begins to explain why and when women became a visible target of the felony law. Felonies were serious crimes that threatened society as a whole. Underlying the origin of the term and all of its progressive redefinitions was the division of crimes into felonies and misdemeanors. Felonies were serious crimes—dangerous, in Hawkins's words, "to the safety of the publick."[22] The earliest category of felonies, treasons or threats to the head of the state, were clearly dangerous, and forfeiture was a fitting penalty for such lese majesty. The addition of the other common law felonies—murder, manslaughter, larceny, robbery, burglary, arson, and jail breaks—came as the crown extended its jurisdiction to the safety and order of the community.[23] The list of statutory felonies grew immense by the middle of the eighteenth century as the lawmakers in Parliament and the colonies began to view threats to new forms of property as acts threatening to society. In the listing of felonies, Wood might vary from Sir Matthew Hale's *Pleas of the Crown,* and Blackstone might both add to and subtract from their accounts, but felonies remained those crimes that authority viewed to be most damaging to social order.[24]

If felony law was, in fact, a rough index of offenses that authorities judged most dangerous to public safety and social order, and if certain actions performed only by or primarily by women began to be viewed as particularly dangerous to society, felony law might well develop a special concern for women. And this is what happened. Early in the English Reformation, the king's county quarter sessions courts began to intrude upon the jurisdiction of the ecclesiastical courts, taking from them jurisdiction over sexual misconducts,[25] cases primarily involving and especially focusing upon women. Shortly thereafter, a campaign waged in the later Elizabethan and early Stuart Parliaments against the wantonness and laziness of the wandering poor resulted in additional laws against all sorts of social misconduct, including sexual acts.[26] A major target of the new statutes was the poor female parent of bastard children. The Poor Law of 1576 decreed that parents of bastard children were perceived as having "defrauded" the parish, by thrusting destitute infants upon local charity, thereby reducing its capacity to relieve the "true poor." The mother was to name the father, and the father was to give a bond or weekly payment to the parish. Noncompliance could result in corporal punishment and jail terms for either parent.[27] Poor mothers almost always faced public disgrace under this act. Fathers drawn from the landless laboring class fled; well-to-do fathers, on occasion the master of the unwed mother, confuted her accusation of paternity.

The attention of the law and the courts thus focused more and more upon the immorality of women. This in itself did not affect felony law, for bastardy and other sexual offenses were not felonies but were punished at the quarter sessions or summarily by single justices.[28] The greater suspicion with which women were viewed and the increasing number of times they were brought into the king's courts nevertheless had consequences beyond increased whippings, fines, and imprisonments for fornication.[29]

One consequence was that felonies that had long applied to both sexes but were previously not discussed in relation to women were now explicitly extended and applied to females.

For example, bestiality, a felony under the common law ordinarily associated with men, was extended explicitly to women by Coke, who wrote that "within the [purview] of this Act of 25 H. 8 sec. 2 the words be, if any person, &c. which extend as well to a woman as to a man," a comment occasioned by the accusation of bestiality against a "great lady" for copulating with a "baboon" and "conceiving by it."[30] Petty treason, long "a Crime where One out of Malice Taketh away the Life of a Subject, To whom He oweth a Special Obedience," was in seventeenth-century law commentaries increasingly associated with women.[31] There were three categories of such breach of obedience: a servant killing his mistress or the wife of his master or his master; a wife killing her husband; and a person in religious orders killing his superior. Children suspected of killing parents were not included, except when the child served the parent for wages, in which case the child was indicted as a servant. When a wife killed her husband, she was thus guilty of petty treason and "if convicted shall be Burned."[32] A husband who killed his wife was guilty of common law murder, and if condemned, he was hanged. This distinction in definition of crime and prescription of punishment between husband-murder and wife-murder became apparent for the first time in the late sixteenth century.

Bestiality and petty treason were crimes whose implications for women were fully discussed in late Elizabethan England, but they were not crimes *created* then. Witchcraft, which became an offense against the crown for the first time in these years, was always a gender-related offense. The English statute law against witchcraft originated in the sixteenth century. Before that time witchcraft—including divining, treasure-finding, fortune-telling, and the casting of spells as well as consorting with the devil—was tried and punished in church courts.[33] New laws in England made the witch a criminal when her actions brought harm to someone or something. This was the *maleficium* without which the English courts would not prosecute (unlike the Continental courts, whose target was religious heresy).[34] Nevertheless, the vast number of cases flooding the English courts— witchcraft accounted for 13 percent of all home circuit assize cases in the 1590s[35]—were primarily directed against women. Over 90 percent of the defendants were female.[36] In truth, many of these women were "cunning folk" and used a form of magic to heal the sick and divine the future. But the accusations went beyond these primitive doctors and soothsayers to include older, poorer women who were disliked and feared by their neighbors.[37] The accusers and the courts believed in the efficacy of magic and, more important, in the malignity of female suspects, whose curses and threats took on reality when a cow or a child sickened and died. Felony law placed the suspected witches in jeopardy of their lives if the apparatus of witchcraft or other evidence proved that they practiced the black arts. By statutes in the reigns of Henry VIII, Edward VI, Elizabeth I, and James I, the uses of magic to cast spells, cause harm, find treasure, and tell the future became felonies. Again, it is not easy to pinpoint the reasons for this great expansion of felony law against women, but the breakdown of older social relationships within medieval villages and the hard times of the 1590s explain some of the accusations against old women.[38]

Unattached poor young women were put under duress by another addition to the felony law. The Stuart infanticide statute of 1624 (21 James I c. 27) made an unmarried mother's concealment of her bastard infant's death presumptive evidence of murder.

> An act to prevent the destroying and murthering of bastard children.
>
> WHEREAS, many lewd women that have been delivered of bastard children, to avoid their shame, and to escape punishment, do secretly bury or conceal the death of their children, and after, if the child be found dead, the said women do alledge, that the said child was born dead; whereas it falleth out sometimes (although hardly it is to be proved) that the said child or children were murthered by the said women, their lewd mothers, or by their assent or procurement:
>
> II. For the preventing therefore of this great mischief, be it enacted by the authority of this present parliament, That if any woman after one month next ensuing the end of this session of parliament be delivered by any issue of her body, male or female, which being born alive, should by the laws of this realm be a bastard, and that she endeavour privately, either by drowning or secret burying thereof, or any other way, either by herself or the procuring of others, so to con-

ceal the death thereof, as that it may not come to light, whether it were born alive or not, but be concealed: in every case the said mother so offending shall suffer death as in case of murther, except such mother can make proof by one witness at the least, that the child (whose death was by her so intended to be concealed) was born dead.[39]

The Jacobean statute of infanticide did not apply to men, to legitimate children, or married women (save those guilty of bearing a bastard under the law), but only to a special class of women. It was a harsh law, and while it did not completely shift the burden of proof onto the defendant, it did give the agents of the crown—particularly those whose personal convictions bent them in this direction already—a powerful tool to prosecute those poor women who, to avoid the stigma and penalities of the bastardy law, secretly buried their stillborn offspring.

The subtle but discernible sharpening of the visibility of women in the felony law was not merely the result of Puritan misogyny—if one could call Puritan social policy misogynous, which one may do only with great caution. Nondissenting English religious and lay authorities were as worried about the homeless woman and her offspring. But the Puritans added a prophetic shrillness to commonly expressed views among the better classes. It was not that Puritan ministers, lawmakers, and justices of peace spent sleepless nights preparing their campaigns against women; they had other, more difficult and more pressing battles to wage. At the same time, the root of Puritan piety lay in a cleanliness of the individual spirit, a continual self-scrutiny, which wanton sexuality corrupted. True, these men were not religious automata—they were husbands and fathers, farmers and craftsmen—but make no mistake: when it came to defining crimes the magistrates and lawmakers of early Massachusetts were Puritans, not merely Congregationalists or New Englanders. They did not separate the facts of crimes from the assumption of sinfulness, which is why they mitigated punishment when given evidence of contrition and repentance. And if they saw certain types of women as especially prone to sin, their laws would seek out and smite the sin behind the crime.[40]

It is not surprising, then, that the first code of laws of the

Massachusetts Bay Colony, promulgated in 1641, and the later *Body of Liberties* (1648) added gender-specific offenses to the list of capital crimes. Most of the criminal code would have been familiar to any educated Englishman or woman, as its entries were derived from the common law of England. The statutory law of crime, primarily relating to offenses against the dignity of the crown, was largely omitted in the *Body of Liberties*, making that document a genuine reform of English practice. To the shortened list of common law crimes, the governor and Court of Assistants of the colony added a handful of offenses drawn from the Bible, including blasphemy (an offense the Puritans took very seriously) and idol worship. In England these were the business of the ecclesiastical courts, which could not take life or limb for a crime, but the Court of Assistants in Massachusetts could order death for these violations of religious law. In point of fact, it never did, but the threat and thus the message hung over the entire population of the colony. To these offenses were added disobedience to parents. Again, the symbolic force of the prohibition over time outweighed any real danger it posed to rebellious youths. Only one case of a child striking a parent even came close to an actual indictment.[41] But this reduction of real crimes to hyperbolic admonitions may be too presentist. Certainly, the punishments for other offenses on the list were meant to be more than symbolic. Murder, manslaughter, poisoning, rape, sodomy, man-stealing, perjury in capital cases, conspiracy to commit treason, and treason were all serious crimes and the laws against them were enforced. The last entry was adultery. In England adultery was an offense against the church, until the Puritans gained control of Parliament; for the duration of the Protectorate of Oliver Cromwell, adultery became a capital offense throughout the realm. The Bay Colony laws anticipated that enactment by a decade.[42]

Women were excluded from the definitions of rape, disobedience to parents, and man-stealing; it was inconceivable to New England lawgivers that women could ever be a party to such crimes. They were included in the crimes of murder, manslaughter, and witchcraft. The article on adultery did not exempt men from punishment, but differentiated between the roles of women and men in the commission of the act. "If any person commit adultery with a married or espoused wife," the article read, that person and the wife would be executed. The only sensible denotation of "person" is "man." The status of the man was unimportant, it was the status of the woman in law that determined the severity of the crime. Lying with a single woman was fornication, a serious misdemeanor. Thus was the double standard read into the highest law of the colony. There is an echo of this in the article defining rape: for a victim under the age of ten, the perpetrator's penalty was death (the result of an earlier case in the colony). If the victim was older, the court could reduce the charge to an assault and punish the accused accordingly. During the years covered by this study, the number of rape convictions was less than ten. The child could not corrupt anyone, but the older woman was the potential temptress. At any rate, rape was a difficult charge to prove before an all-male jury.[43]

The practical effect of these deviations from the criminal law of England was not felt equally by the two sexes: the differences favored the men. Offenses such as robbery and burglary, which were capital crimes in England, were not capital in Massachusetts until the third offense. In the Bay Colony first offenses of burglary, for example, were punished with branding, fines, and damages (restitution included) and second offenses with whipping.[44] Lesser thefts, still capital crimes in England, resulted in fines and payment of double or treble damages.[45] The reduction of penalty for these offenses did ease the pain of law for men because the bulk of burglaries, robberies, and other offenses against property were committed by men. Men roamed the market towns, traveled the roads, were abroad at night, and drove carts—all aids to the illegal taking and transporting of others' goods. Women committed these offenses with minor frequency (compared to men) throughout the colonial period. On the other hand, women did not fare so well under other deviations from English law. In particular, adultery was made a capital crime in the Bay Colony; in England (except for the Protectorate) it remained a matter for the ecclesiastical courts.[46] Adulteries had by definition at least one female culprit, a far higher proportion of female to male defendants (1 to 1) than in all but two other crimes—witchcraft and infanticide. And the adultery provisions of the 1648 code were enforced. In 1644 Mary Latham and James Britton were executed for committing adultery. She had cuckolded her aged husband and publicly admitted it.[47] The Court of Assistants took such untoward boasting very seriously, as it did all evidences of adulterous conduct. Here was, however, the first and only execution for this offense. Between 1673 and 1774 there were thirty-eight indictments for adultery heard in the highest courts, thirty of which were against women. Punishment was meted out with the rod and at the pillory. Convicts also stood upon the gallows with halters about their necks. For a time, the law also prescribed the wearing of a letter "A"—Nathaniel Hawthorne's *Scarlet Letter*.[48]

The addition of adultery to the list of capital offenses in 1648 was even more significant than the actual ratio of female/male prosecutions over the entire colonial period indicates, because of the symbolic influence of the new law. Adultery was regarded as a cumulative crime in its origin, the result of lesser offenses of wanton and lascivious behavior amounting to seduction. The Massachusetts criminal code of 1648 was promulgated in the Bay Colony after eighteen years of cases and judgments in the Court of Assistants, time enough for the magistrates there (who also sat as the colonial council) to realize that offenses against sexual mores had crossed the Atlantic despite the social conservatism of the Puritan founders. Numerous among the cases heard in these sessions were alleged episodes of "lewd and lascivious carriage," "wanton daliance," "incontinence," "fornication," and "cohabitation." The concern of a society with any set of events may be measured in part by the number of terms its members use to describe that event. The Eskimos, for example, have over a hundred words for different types of snow. If the verbal creativity of the first magistrates is any evidence, the leaders of the Bay Colony found sexual misbehavior very important indeed. The courts punished suspects in these cases without hesitation; only a few of the accused escaped any penalty.[49] While many of the accusations may have been based upon fact, the degree and speed of punishment suggest that the crimes themselves were so threatening to the authorities that mere suspicion had to lead to formal

action. And, most important for this discussion, the preponderance of these crimes of sexual misconduct were gender-
related, that is, the presentment or indictment was directed
against women.[50]

Proportionately more women were named in these cases
than for any other lesser offense. Though fathers of bastard
newborns were fined, mothers were beaten and shamed, so
that bastardy laws worked to the special disadvantage of
women. As the Massachusetts court system developed and
county courts emerged, cases of bastardy, fornication, and
lewd conduct filled the county dockets. In the Essex and Suffolk county courts between 1671 and 1674, fornication cases
were the most numerous of any crime category.[51] Ministers
and judges in the Bay Colony may or may not have regarded
women as the instigators and temptors of men in these crimes,
but using Eve and Bathsheba as their texts, Increase and Cotton Mather and their ministerial brethren made clear that
women's fornication led to more serious crimes and a general
breakdown of social order.[52]

As the highest courts in the colony devoted so much time
and energy in these early years to the correction of "unclean"
women, the justices fretted about the purity of their New
World sanctuary. While still in England, the Puritans had been
among the most vigorous condemnors of the sins of the
flesh.[53] To the Puritan leaders of the Bay Colony, such crimes
were as threatening as treason had been to the Norman and
Angevin kings of England. It is not surprising, then, to find as
much concern for deviant women in the felony law of the
Massachusetts Bay Colony as there was concern for political
and religious plotters in the felony law of Elizabethan and
Stuart England. As women accused of gender-related offenses
received more attention and seemed particularly threatening,
so women became a visible object of the felony lawmakers and
the criminal court judges who interpreted that law. The eleva-
tion of adultery to the category of capital crimes embodied the
Puritan's detestation of such offenses and provided, in theory,
a powerful deterrent to such crimes.[54]

Are these alterations in the criminal code evidence of ir-
reconcilable Puritan misogyny? Lyle Koehler is the most recent in a long line of historians who answer affirmatively. For

Koehler, the law was a pervasive and authoritative reminder that women were subordinate creatures. If Puritan culture was misogynistic, "covering law" theory would conclude that Puritan criminal law would also be misogynistic. This is neither adequate logic nor valid history. As a host of historians of Puritan domestic life have demonstrated, individual Puritan fathers, husbands, and sons loved and respected women in their families and communities. How can the indisputable evidence of female subordination be aligned with the overwhelming evidence of affection and esteem for individual women in the same society? One must be wary of reasoning from extremes, but the treatment of women accused of witchcraft affords the beginning of an answer to the puzzle. As John Demos has demonstrated in exquisite detail in *Entertaining Satan,* attribution of witchery to individual women did not proceed from a generalized misogyny, but from complex mixtures of psychological tension and distrust, sociological alienation, and community disruption particular to each case.[55] That is, there was potential for misogyny, but strong antifeminine feelings did not cause women to be questioned or arraigned for supposed acts of *maleficium.* The witchcraft laws applied to men as well as women, and a handful of men (less than 10 percent of the total named) were indicted for the crime. Everyone in Puritan New England understood that the real target of the witchcraft laws were witches, not warlocks or "cunning men." Here is the key in beginning to understand the relationship between the code and the treatment of women: community attitudes were not a product of enforcement of law, that is, of its punitive reality, but of its admonitory capacity. One must bear in mind that the Puritans were an admonitory people: the sermon was a popular form of communication; the religious tract was a common genre of academic discourse; the language of statutes and other governmental pronouncements was always admonitory. The criminal code shared this property: it was meant to have a preventive and uplifting effect. The Puritans knew that crime was inevitable, as inevitable as backsliding in matters of faith, but their laws were a statement of principles just the same. And often as not, some way was found to mitigate the absolute severity of the laws when the suspect proffered sincere contrition. Thus, as we will see,

33

adulterous acts were reduced to charges of wanton dalliance, lascivious conduct, or another nonfelonious offense, and the same process saved women (and men) from the full rigor of the other capital laws. The potential for misogyny was there, but it was not the force behind the criminal laws.

The end of the seventeenth century saw the beginning of a retreat from intense concern with the preceptual conjunction of gender, sin, and crime in Massachusetts.[56] Between the code of 1648 and the end of the colonial period, felony law in the Bay Colony was altered visibly. The pace of change was slow, and the basic outlines of the law did not vary drastically, but the changes did improve the status of women. Capital offenses in 1672 were the same as those in 1648.[57] In 1692 the General Court submitted a revised list for Privy Council approval under the new charter. Arson and piracy were added to treason, murder, sodomy, bestiality, concealment of suspiciously dead bastard infants, incest, and rape as felonies deserving of death.[58] When the Privy Council disallowed the act in 1695, the General Court submitted individual statutes rather than a code to the English authorities. In a series of acts, murder, piracy, treason, infanticide, rape, bestiality, and—in the 1710s—burglary and highway robbery were made capital offenses, the latter two with benefit of clergy (until legislation in 1772 removed that plea).[59] Witchcraft ceased to be a capital offense when the General Court failed to resubmit it under a separate statute.[60] Adultery remained a felony, but the penalty for conviction was reduced to a whipping,[61] and cases were rarely heard in the superior courts. Maternal neonaticides were still governed by the guidelines of 1624, which were passed in Massachusetts in 1696, but conviction upon evidence of concealment alone became increasingly rare: only one case in twenty after 1730.

Felonies, those crimes most dangerous to society, now included the sophisticated larcenies of a commercial, paper instrument–oriented society. Statutes prohibited varieties of forgery, counterfeiting, passing counterfeit deeds, bills of credit, and currency, and other forms of fraud, embezzlement, and larceny.[62] Perpetrators of such crimes, most of them men, were dangerous to a modern mercantile society.[63] The men of commercial substance and material goals who now made the laws did not fear wanton or unruly women so much as ministers and laymen had.[64]

This is not to say that felony law as a whole became more lenient toward women or that women were not apprehended, tried, and convicted under the new felony laws against counterfeiting and forgery. When burglary and highway robbery became capital offenses upon a first conviction, women were placed in as much jeopardy as men. The point is that these alterations in the felony law were not designed with women as targets, that is, with crimes usually associated with women.

Indeed, women retained traditional defenses against some felony charges throughout the colonial period.[65] In August 1766, for example, the court dismissed charges of felonious theft against Mary Hodges, the wife of Richard, and Mary Clark, the wife of John, because they were *femes covert*. Their husbands, both mariners, were convicted.[66] In defense of herself against a charge of theft, Margaret Knodle tried to plead that the goods belonged to her husband, Frederick. The jury found the plea inadequate, for Margaret committed the crime "while she was sole and before her intermarriage with the said Frederick Knodle."[67] Women evidently were apprised of this anomaly in the felony law. The survival of *feme covert* was not, however, an unmixed blessing: while it afforded women some relief in the criminal courts, it insured their subservience to their husbands on the civil side of the law.[68]

At the end of the century women gained benefit of clergy in felony trials. This was originally applicable to men in lesser religious offices and by the seventeenth century had been extended to all male first offenders in a variety of felonies who could "read the book."[69] That is, the death sentence could be averted by the convict's reading of the 51st or "neck" psalm, and the defendant was branded or otherwise marked and dismissed. Murder, treason, and a number of other serious offenses were not subject to this device, but most offenses against property, manslaughter, and many lesser felonies were still clergyable. The "statute of Jacobi" (21 James I. c. 6) of 1624—"That on a Conviction of Grand Larceny, under the Value of 10s, being no Burglary, nor Robbery in or near the Highway, nor a felonious private taking from the Person, &c. but only such as Offense for which a Man might have his

Clergy, they [women] shall be burnt in the Hand, and imprisoned, &c."—gave to women benefit of clergy in lesser offenses
against property.[70] This English reform was not concerned
with crimes growing out of women's sexual misconduct but
applied to them when they committed crimes generally attempted by men. Women in Massachusetts apparently did not
plead nor receive benefit of clergy until a later reform in England. In England, after 1624, women were still not entitled to
clergy for manslaughters. Justice Michael Foster and others in
the mid-eighteenth century considered this omission harsh and
applauded the extension of clergy to women "in all clergyable
offenses" under the 1692 statute of 3 and 4 William and Mary
c. 9, par. 7.[71] Foster reasoned that women should particularly
be afforded clergy for manslaughter because "women, were
from the Delicacy of their Frame . . . most susceptible of Human Passions."[72] This statute was received in Massachusetts
Bay, and female felons in its courts were spared.

Felony law changed with the changing priorities of the
men who made all law. As the offenses of women, and within
those the offenses peculiar to women and committed primarily by women, became less worrisome, and other crimes
against mercantile paper, and other instruments—crimes
damaging to fiscal policy—became more important, the emphasis of the felony law shifted. Was there also a softening of
men's hearts toward women? As the criminal law shifted,
women's criminality had to shift as well, for the former
created the occasion for the latter. By examining the pattern
of recorded female crime, we can probe the question of bias
from a second perspective. This is our next objective.

NOTES

1. Roscoe Pound, *An Introduction to the Philosophy of Law* (New Haven,
Conn., 1954), 29, but note that Pound regards "dominance" as an economic
or political question.

2. William Blackstone, *Commentaries on the Laws of England*, 4 vols.
(Oxford, 1759–65), 1:54. *Malum in se* crimes imply that the suspect intended
to harm or to do evil; see Kenneth M. Wells and Paul B. Weston, *Criminal
Law* (Santa Monica, Calif., 1978), 109–10, and Joseph Keble, *An Assistance to
Justices of the Peace . . .* (London, 1683), 239.

3. The modern version of the concept is that criminal behavior is "behavior in violation of criminal law"; see E. H. Sutherland and D. R. Cressey, *Criminology*, 10th ed. (Philadelphia, 1978), 4. This may seem an extremely relativistic position, but criminal law does recognize *malum prohibitum* as valid. On the labeling of female prostitutes, see Marshall B. Clinard and Robert F. Meier, *The Sociology of Deviant Behavior*, 5th ed. (New York, 1979), 406–8.

4. Over time, *mala prohibita* offenses may change a good deal, as different groups' behavior becomes more threatening to the dominant groups in a society. On the labeling of socioeconomic, racial, and ethnic groups as deviants, see Sue Titus Reid, *Crime and Criminology* (Duxbury, Mass., 1977), 58–61. Certain behaviors of individuals (who may be of different ethnic or socioeconomic backgrounds) may also be labeled as "deviant" and, if their actions are threatening to dominant values, may be made criminal.

5. Richard West, *A Discourse Concerning Treasons* (London, 1717), 19; William Nelson, *Office and Authority of a Justice of Peace* (London, 1729), 284; Blackstone, *Commentaries*, 4:95.

6. Blackstone, *Commentaries*, 4:374.

7. T. F. T. Plucknett, *A Concise History of the Common Law*, 5th ed. (Boston, 1956), 442.

8. Edward Coke, *The First Part of the Institutes of the Laws of England*, 4th ed. (London, 1669), 391.

9. Giles Jacob, *The Student's Companion: or, The Reasons of the Laws of England* (London, 1725), 57; Thomas Wood, *An Institute of the Laws of England* (London, 1722), 347.

10. See Blackstone, *Commentaries*, 4:101, for example, an embezzlement of the king's war supplies.

11. Barbara Hanawalt, "The Female Felon in Fourteenth-Century England," *Viator* 5 (1974), 259.

12. James B. Given, *Society and Homicide in Thirteenth-Century England* (Stanford, 1977), 135.

13. William Hawkins, *A Treatise on the Pleas of the Crown*, 2 vols. (London, 1716), 1:65.

14. Michael Dalton, *The Countrey Justice* (London, 1622), 42.

15. Blackstone, *Commentaries*, 4:98.

16. Ralph B. Pugh, *Wiltshire Gaol Delivery and Trailbaston Trials, 1275–1306* (Devizes, 1978), 38.

17. Blackstone, *Commentaries*, 1:442.

18. Coke, *Third Part of the Institute*, 110.

19. Ibid., 108.

20. Wood, *Institute*, 341. The "presumption" of coercion was overruled at last in *People v. Stately*, 1949, a California appellate court decision discussed in Leo Kanowitz, *Sex Roles in Law and Society: Cases and Materials* (Albuquerque, 1973), 258–62.

21. Any strict definition of felony based solely upon either forfeiture or evil intent or capital punishment is inadequate. For example, Michael Foster reported that manslaughter has a "felonious result" that need not

have arisen from evil intent. See his *A Report on Some Proceedings . . . of Oyer and Terminer* (Oxford, 1762), 290. Manslaughter was usually classed among the common law felonies, although William Nelson excluded "involuntary" homicides from felony because they did not have an evil intent (*Justice of Peace*, 285). Nevertheless, as Thomas Wood noted, "in Chancemedley, the Offender Forfeits His Goods, but Hath a Pardon of Course" (*Institute*, 358). This presents the case of an offense "not properly a felony" that had forfeiture as its automatic punishment! Manslaughter was clergyable and so did not usually result in execution. Sir William Blackstone reported that "felony may be without inflicting capital punishment, as in the cases instanced of self-murder, excusable homicide, and petty larceny: and it is possible that capital punishments may be inflicted and yet the offense be no felony; as in the case of heresy by the common law, which, though capital, never worked any forfeiture of lands or goods, an inseparable incident to felony" (*Commentaries*, 4:97). Indeed, standing mute in preference to pleading to felony was itself a felony, but it averted forfeiture.

22. Hawkins, *Pleas of the Crown*, 1:preface.

23. Blackstone, *Commentaries*, 4:95–96.

24. Nelson, *Justice of Peace*, 285–92, named felonies under several heads: forgery, counterfeiting, theft-by-tricks, concealing the death of a bastard, buggery (bestiality included), destruction of another's property over a certain value, mayhem, frauds, hunting the king's deer, aiding the Jesuits, bigamy, rape, embezzlement, burning ships, barns, and corn, wartime desertion by soldiers, the return to England of outlaws or transported felons, witchcraft (of either first or second degrees), kidnapping, forced marriage, and wrecking ships, in addition to the older felonies of burglary, robbery, treason, murder, and manslaughter.

25. Ralph Houlbrook, *Church Courts and the People during the English Reformation, 1520–1570* (Oxford, 1979), 79.

26. See Joan R. Kent, "Attitudes of Members of the House of Commons to the Regulation of 'Personal Conduct' in Late Elizabethan and Early Stuart England," *Bulletin of the Institute of Historical Research* 46 (May 1973), 41–71.

27. 18 Eliz. I c. 3 (1576).

28. William Lambard, "Charge to the Quarter Session after Easter, 1586," and Lambard, "An Ephemeris," both in *William Lambard and Local Government*, ed. Conyers Read (Ithaca, N.Y., 1962), 85, 30; Thomas G. Barnes, *Somerset, 1625–1640: A County's Government during the 'Personal Rule'* (Cambridge, Mass., 1961), 62; Peter Laslett, *The World We Have Lost* (New York, 1965), 135. On court cases involving bastardy, see also J. S. Furley, *Quarter Session Government in Hampshire in the Seventeenth Century* (Winchester, 1937), 70–71, and S. A. Peyton, ed., *Minutes of Proceedings in Quarter Session . . . in the County of Lincoln* (Lincoln, 1931), cix.

29. For example, the consequences were felt in infanticide prosecutions; see Peter C. Hoffer and N. E. H. Hull, *Murdering Mothers: Infanticide in England and New England, 1558–1803* (New York, 1981), 12–22.

30. Coke, *Third Part of the Institute*, 59.

31. Wood, *Institute*, 346.

32. Foster, *Report*, 323.

33. See George L. Kittredge, *Witchcraft in Old and New England* (rept. ed., New York, 1958), for a discussion of witchcraft in Old and New England.

34. These English statutes against witches are discussed in Wallace Notestein, *A History of Witchcraft in England* (Washington, D.C., 1911), 11ff. English prosecutions did not have all of the erotic, misogynistic overtones of French and German cases.

35. J. S. Cockburn, *A History of the English Assizes, 1558–1714* (Cambridge, 1972), 98.

36. Data are from C. L'estrange Ewen, *Witch Hunting and Witch Trials* (London, 1929).

37. Alan D. Macfarlane, *Witchcraft in Tudor and Stuart England* (New York, 1970), 244–49.

38. This should be compared with a similar argument in David T. Konig, *Law and Society in Puritan Massachusetts: Essex County, 1629–1692* (Chapel Hill, N.C., 1979), 176–77. Konig sees social disorder at the root of the witchcraft accusations.

39. 21 James I c. 27 (1624). On the number of cases, see Hoffer and Hull, *Murdering Mothers,* 7 (Table 1.1).

40. This point, for witchcraft at least, is made very nicely in Richard Weisman, *Witchcraft, Magic, and Religion in Seventeenth-Century Massachusetts* (Amherst, Mass., 1984), 23–29, and given general support in John M. Murrin, "Trial by Jury in Seventeenth-Century New England," in *Saints and Revolutionaries,* ed. David D. Hall et al. (New York, 1984), 193. But see also Barbara A. Black, "The Judicial Power and the General Court in Early Massachusetts" (Ph.D. diss., Yale University, 1975), 189–90.

41. For Porter's case, see John Noble et al., eds., *Records of the Court of Assistants of the Colony of Massachusetts Bay, 1629–1692,* 3 vols. (Boston, 1901–28), 3:138–39 (Mar. 4, 1663), hereafter cited as *Court of Assistants.* For Gridley's case, see ibid., 144–45 (Aug. 1664).

42. The Adultery Law of 1650, though juries were very lenient in these cases.

43. John D. Cushing, ed. and comp., *The Laws and Liberties of Massachusetts, 1641–1691,* 3 vols. (Wilmington, Del., 1976), for 1648, 5–6, hereafter cited as *Laws and Liberties,* followed by the year in parentheses.

44. Ibid., 6. This punishment was not changed until 1714.

45. Ibid., 5.

46. Paul Hair, ed., *Before the Bawdy Court* (London, 1972), 99–100, for example.

47. *Court of Assistants,* 2:139.

48. Carol F. Lee, "Discretionary Justice in Early Massachusetts," *Essex Institute Historical Collections* 112 (Apr. 1976), 130; Edwin Powers, *Crime and Punishment in Early Massachusetts, 1620–1692* (Boston, 1966); Murrin, "Trial by Jury," 190–91.

49. See *Court of Assistants,* 2:19, 30, 32, 60, 66, 70, 72, 81, 87, 90, 91,

92, 93, 94, 95, 107, 121, 124, 137 ("having gotten a *slut* with child") my italics, and Zechariah Chafee, Jr., introduction to the *Records of the Suffolk County Court, 1671–1680,* Publications of the Colonial Society of Massachusetts (Boston, 1933), 29:xvii–xciii.

50. On gender- or sex- specific offenses, see Carol Smart, *Women, Crime and Criminology: A Feminist Critique* (London, 1976), 6. Also see the discussion in Lois J. Frankel, "Sex Discrimination in the Criminal Law: The Effects of the Equal Rights Amendment," *American Criminal Law Review* 2 (Winter 1973), 469–73.

51. See Powers, *Crime and Punishment,* 404–5.

52. See, for example, Cotton Mather's *The Folly of Sinning* (Boston, 1699) and his *Pillars of Salt* (Boston, 1699, both "execution" sermons in cases of women's capital offenses, and pp. ooo–oo in ch. 6 herein.

53. John Downame, *The Christian Warfare* (London, 1604), 39, 101–4; Hannibal Gamon, *Gods Smiting to Amendment . . .* (London, 1628), 28; William Perkins, *The Whole Treatise of the Case of Conscience* (ca. 1596), in Thomas F. Merrill, ed., *William Perkins, 1558–1602* (The Hague, 1966), 106–7ff.; William Gouge, *Of Domestical Duties* (London, 1602), 499–500; Samuel Burton, *A Sermon Preached at the General Assizes in Warwick* (London, 1620), 12–13.

54. The *concept* of felony and the *term* felony were not mentioned in the codes of laws produced in 1641 and 1648 in the Bay Colony. Offenses were instead labeled "capital." Nevertheless, even before the first code of 1641 was passed, the Court of Assistants used and understood, to a limited degree, the concept of felony. In 1633 "John Sayle being convicted of fellonyously takeing away corne & fishe from dyvers persons the laste year , . . is censured by the Court after this manner: That all his estates shalbe forfeited out of wch double restitution shalbe made to those whome hee hath wronged and he shalbe whipt & bound as a servt with any that will retaine him for 3 yeares & after to be disposed of by the Court, as they shall thinke meete" (*Court of Assistants,* 2:32). The felony was punished with a forfeiture. Theft was not a capital offense, but then first or second offenses of theft never were in the Bay Colony. In 1635 a "notorious" thief, Robert Scarlett, recently emigrated to the colony, was severely whipped, branded on the forehead with a T, and expelled after conviction for "diverse felonyes" (ibid., 60). That same year "the Court hath enjoyned William Wills to pay to Gyles Gibbs the some of xvjs [16s.] for ffellony by him committed" (ibid., 56). The word felony continued to be used in the courts throughout the seventeenth century, though it was not mentioned in the laws. In 1694 Benjamin Chubb was found guilty of "theft and fellony" in the Superior Court of Judicature and sentenced to pay John Williams "trebel damages." See the Records of the Superior Court of Judicature, Suffolk County Courthouse, Boston, 1:112, hereafter cited as SCJ. For the most part, the authorities applied the term felony to serious property crimes. This assimilation of felony law is not surprising, for the General Court had ordered copies of the works of Michael Dalton, Edward Coke, and Fernando Pulton on the laws of England for the use of the assistants in 1647. See Nathaniel Shurtleff, ed., *Records of the Governor and Company of the Massachusetts Bay,* 4 vols. (Boston, 1852–64), 2:212.

55. John Putnam Demos, *Entertaining Satan: Witchcraft and the Culture of Early New England* (New York, 1983), 368–86.

56. Changes in this decade of crisis (1690–1700) led to an altered view of state authority. See David D. Damerall, "The Modernization of Massachusetts: The Transformation of Public Attitudes and Institutions, 1689–1715" (Ph.D. diss., University of Texas, 1981), 254–55.

57. See *The General Laws and Liberties of the Massachusetts Colony: Revised and Reprinted* (Cambridge, Mass., 1672), 14–15.

58. *Acts and Resolves, Public and Private, of the Province of Massachusetts Bay,* 21 vols. (Boston, 1869–1922), 1:55–56 (1692), hereafter cited as *Acts and Resolves.*

59. Ibid., 255 (1696), 296–97 (1697), 556 (1704), 577 (1705), 673–74 (1711); 2:5 (1715). For an end to the practice of benefit of clergy in burglary, see ibid., 5:43 (1770).

60. Ibid., 1:55 (1692), disallowed by Privy Council, and not revived; see also Powers, *Crime and Punishment,* 508.

61. *Acts and Resolves,* 1:171 (1694); 4:622 (1763).

62. Counterfeiting and forgery were the sophisticated property crimes most frequently dealt with in the five volumes of *Acts and Resolves* covering the colonial period.

63. See Richard Bushman, *From Puritan to Yankee* (Cambridge, Mass., 1968), 287; Bernard Bailyn, *The New England Merchants in the Seventeenth Century* (New York, 1964), 195; and pp. 62–63 herein.

64. Kai T. Erikson, *Wayward Puritans: A Study in the Sociology of Deviance* (New York, 1966), for example, 100–102; John Demos, "Underlying Themes in the Witchcraft of Seventeenth-Century New England," *American Historical Review* 75 (1970), 1326; Lyle Koehler, "The Case of the American Jezebels: Anne Hutchinson and Female Agitation during the Years of Antinomian Turmoil, 1636–1640," *William and Mary Quarterly,* 3d ser., 31 (1974), 55–78.

65. Richard B. Morris, *Studies in the History of American Law,* 2d ed. (New York, 1958), 200; Alexander Keyssar, "Widowhood in Eighteenth-Century Massachusetts: A Problem in the History of the Family," *Perspectives in American History* 8 (1974), 118.

66. Hodges's and Clark's cases, SCJ 1766–67, 109–10 (Aug. 26, 1766), in Suffolk County Court Files, Suffolk County Courthouse, Boston, vol. 507, #87106, 132, hereafter cited as Suffolk court files.

67. Knodle's case, SCJ 1764–65, 123–24 (Aug. 22, 1764), and Suffolk court files, vol. 578, #100818, 41.

68. Morris, *Studies in the History of American Law,* 126–200; Roger Thompson, *Women in Stuart England and America: A Comparative Study* (London, 1974), 161–68.

69. Blackstone, *Commentaries,* 4:358–67.

70. Hawkins, *Pleas of the Crown,* 2:339.

71. 2 and 4 William and Mary, c. 9 section 7 (1698).

72. Foster, *Report,* 305.

CHAPTER THREE

THE EXTENT OF WOMEN'S FELONY

If the most important crimes were also the most common crimes, historians of crime would be preoccupied with broken fences, fornication, and unexcused absences from church. Frequency does not automatically signify importance. The most common offenses in colonial Massachusetts were simple fornication, name-calling (slander), assault (threatened physical injury) with or without battery, and disorderly conduct.[1] While some of these were handled in church courts, on other occasions disputes among individuals and families were brought to the civil courts. County courts heard and disposed of the accusations of incontinence, assault, and other petty offenses.[2] Single justices of the peace, out of session, could also deal with minor offenses.[3] Unruly women and sexually active women were far more common than felonious women, but allowing the former to obscure the latter also obscures the distinct questions of felony prosecutions of women: what kinds of serious crimes did women commit, how often did they commit these crimes, and how was their conduct distinguished from that of male offenders? A certain amount of disorder in a society may be expected; no one, even a Puritan, was shocked or surprised that women shouted obscenities at their neighbors or raised a hand to each other. But women who murdered, robbed, and burgled, or who abetted murders, robbers, and burglars, caused anger and fear among their neighbors.

Unfortunately, in this era before crimes were reported regularly, when court records are often the closest the scholar can get to the commission of crimes, the simplest questions to frame can become the hardest to answer. How many serious crimes did women commit? At what rate (that is, in what proportion to the female population who could commit serious crimes) did they commit these crimes? How did the rate change over time? And how did it compare with rates for men? Basic questions—to be sure—but they are technically difficult, requiring extrapolation from the court record, assumptions about the distribution of the data, and a number of educated guesses about the "dark" figure of crimes.

"Dark" figures are the nightmare of students of historical as well as contemporary crime. In colonial Massachusetts, as in America today, not every crime is reported to authorities, and not every report is investigated. Some rumors and accusations were dismissed by Bay Colony constables, magistrates, and other officials out of hand. These accusations thus remain unknown. A justice of the peace, sitting in the county, was not a court of record when he heard reports of offenses. He might order a constable to detain a suspect or bring a witness before him but make no written record. Only when he bound a suspect over for indictment, ordered witnesses to appear, and took testimony for the benefit of the grand jurors at the principal criminal courts did he commit himself to the pen. In colonial Massachusetts the number of minor or petty crimes never recorded may be very large indeed.

If the problem of the dark figures of crime is inescapable in any study of criminal justice and becomes more acute as the scholar travels back in time, evidence points to the likelihood that, overall, changes in crimes recorded vary directly with changes in the number of crimes actually committed.[4] In addition, the more serious a crime, the more likely it was, and is, to be reported. This is logical; the victim or community tends to report those crimes that threaten lives and property.[5] Any corpse found under suspicious cicrumstances called forth a coroners' inquest, at which a jury heard evidence and reached a conclusion on the cause of death. Theft of goods, breaking and entering, robbery, and arson were not overlooked by victims. Revenge, an alternative to pressing a claim in criminal court, was evidently not a common event in the Bay Colony. Both men and women took their serious complaints to the courts.[6]

The law provided for the report of men's and women's crimes in the same fashion. The same officers of the court, justices of the peace, and grand jurors heard accusations against both sexes. A review of the steps by which a suspect was identified, interrogated, and indicted shows the potential for prejudice, but does not establish a consistent pattern for translating the potentiality into actuality.

Distribution of Crimes

Even a glance at the number and percentage of types of crimes that were recorded in the Superior Court ledgers reveals that women were charged with a wide variety of serious crimes. Strikingly, murder and manslaughter accounted for 34 percent of female felonies, more than twice the percentage of any other crime, while witchcraft and sexual offenses (incest, bestiality, bigamy, and adultery) together added another 31 percent to the total. Women were charged with serious assaults and property crimes such as burglary, felonious stealing, and counterfeiting far less frequently. (See Table 1.)

TABLE 1. Serious Female Crime, by Case, in Massachusetts, 1673–1774

Crime	Number	Percentage
Murder/manslaughter	77	34.4
Witchcraft	34	15.2
Adultery	30	13.4
Incest/buggery/bigamy	6	2.7
Arson	8	3.6
Burglary/felonious stealing/breaking and entering	33	14.7
Counterfeiting/uttering counterfeit currency	11	4.9
Assault	8	3.6
Other personal	8	3.6
Other property	9	4.0
Total	224	100.1[a]

[a]The total is greater than 100 percent due to rounding.

Women's crimes in total and by type were not distributed evenly within the geographic boundaries of the colony. By far the largest number—107—came before the court when it sat in Boston for the county of Suffolk. The number of female felons in each county declined the farther it was from the capital. Table 2 shows the number of women defendants brought before the court in the various counties between the years 1673 and 1774.

TABLE 2. Number of Women Brought before the
Highest Courts of Massachusetts for Serious
Offenses, by County in Which the Court Sat,
1673–1774

County	Number of Women Accused
Suffolk	107
Essex	40
Middlesex	23
Worcester	11
Plymouth	10
Barnstable	10
Bristol	10
Hampshire/Berkshire	8
York	2
Cumberland/Lincoln	2
Nantucket Island	1

The pattern of prosecution among the counties is more or less what one might expect from the relative density of population and way of life. The character of these counties predicates somewhat the nature of female crimes. Suffolk, for example, was the mercantile center of the colony, and the largest proportion of its female crimes—78 percent—were thefts, larcenies, and other offenses against property; 27 percent of these were more sophisticated property offenses: forgery, counterfeiting, and passing counterfeit currency. Rural counties had more crimes against persons than against property, typical in traditional rural settings.[7] The Essex sessions, which included Salem, had a preponderance of crimes against persons, almost 65 percent of which were witchcraft cases. The next largest categories were homicide, 22.5 percent; sexual/morals offenses, 7.5 percent; and smaller property crimes, 5 percent. The largest category of serious female offense heard in Middlesex was homicide (34.8 percent of the cases), but more than a quarter of all cases were assaults (26.1 percent), a fifth were simple property offenses, and a small percentage were sexual/morals offenses (16.1 percent). The remaining counties had patterns of serious female crime similar to Middlesex; crimes against persons dominated the court's business, with a smattering of property and sexual/morals offenses. The counties of Barnstable, Hampshire, Berkshire, and Bristol all heard a small but significantly higher number of sophisticated property offenses, including counterfeiting, altering currency, and the passing of such currency. Perhaps these counties, because of their proximity to Rhode Island, New Hampshire, or Connecticut, saw more passing of false currency because they had a greater mixture of currencies. Or perhaps in these less populated areas people who attempted to use counterfeit or altered paper money were more easily detected. One other significant geographical aberration was the number of sexual/morals offenses prosecuted in Worcester—five of the crimes heard when the court held its sessions in the county. A rural area for most of this time, Worcester had more than its share of adultery and incest cases. It was the only county in which the number of sexual/morals prosecutions exceeded homicides. While the actual numbers of cases were quite small, and a prudent historian might stop here, it could also be proposed that regulation of morality was less successfully handled by informal social controls in so sparsely settled a region, and the court had to be called upon to discipline the miscreants. Other frontier counties had perhaps too few women for this pattern to emerge.

In almost every one of the counties mentioned, homicide led all other categories of indictments of women for serious crimes. This fact has a social foundation. Crime is a reflection of social opportunities. The limited sphere for women in colonial society, largely confined to the home, resulted in crimes related to their domestic role.[8] Broader economic opportunities were rare, so economic crimes were rare; personal violence, particularly directed at family, was more frequent.[9] Eighty-four percent of the victims in cases of female criminal homicide were children of the accused. The high rate of infanticide suggests that women's violent crimes were directed often against the only people over whom women had control—their children. Some women undoubtedly rid themselves of unwanted bastard newborns to avoid the shame and financial burdens of bastardy. Cotton Mather's maid, for example, was turned out of her place for being suspected of bearing a bastard. Infanticide indictments suggest as well that male authorities were sensitive to this area of female deviant behavior and responded with indictments whenever such cases were suspected. Infanticide and child murder struck at the foundations of the domestic roles of women and the structure of the family.[10]

Although women's homicides were primarily committed against their own children, other targets were masters and neighbors. In the 1750s two black women servants named Phillis, one in Suffolk and the other in Middlesex, were tried for homicides directed at their masters' families.[11] Phillis of Boston killed the grandson of her apothecary master. Phillis of Charlestown killed her master, John Codman. When victims were not babies and masters, they were neighboring children, other women, and relatives. In 1694 Katherine Ford was acquitted of a charge of murder when, probably in the heat of anger, she pushed widow Pheby White down the steps of Ann Pierce's Boston shop.[12] In 1735 Patience, a Falmouth Indian woman, pushed the eight-year-old son of a neighbor into a well.[13] And in 1769 Elizabeth Eams was indicted with her two grown children for poisoning Ruth Eams, probably an elderly relative, with white arsenic.[14] Women used many weapons. In order of frequency they were: drowning, beating (of children), starvation and neglect, poison, axes and knives, and clubs or guns. Because most female homicides were against children, physical strength was not necessary. Drowning, strangling, smothering, and exposure were the most common methods (twenty-six of fifty-one cases), all of which were easily accomplished by the average woman. Both Phillises used poison. Otto Pollak, among others, identifies poison as a particularly female weapon, an attribute of women's "secretive and devious" character.[15] This view has come under attack by social role theorists who logically argue that women seize the weapons available to them. Poisoning food was consistent with women's roles as homemakers or maidservants and required little physical strength. Phillis, the apothecary's servant, had access to poisonous compounds. The other Phillis had a male

accomplice who was the servant of a Middlesex apothecary.
And it was not totally unknown for a man to use poison.
Adam McNeal, a Charlestown mariner, was charged with
killing his wife, Dorothy, with mercury sublimate in 1762.[16]
Nevertheless, men, physically stronger and accustomed to fire-
arms, most frequently shot or bludgeoned their murder victims; they rarely used poison. Elizabeth Remington, who used
a knife to slit the throat of her three-month-old son, was one
of the two female murderers who used a knife or gun.[17] In
the only case in which a woman was accused of murder with a
gun, Martha Throop, a Bristol spinster, was charged in 1720
with shooting Flora, an Indian woman. The grand jury rejected the charge and returned the bill "ignoramus."[18] The
male grand jurors may have concluded that Throop accident-
ally fired the weapon. To prevent any further fatal misadven-
tures, the court ordered the sheriff to take possession of
Throop's gun "for his majesty's use."[19]

The role theory of female homicides posits that women
kill in the home or near it, while men take life in the streets
and taverns. File papers and indictment entries do show that
women killed their victims in bedrooms, attics, kitchens, and
the grounds immediately around their dwellings. Men slew
their victims in or near their houses in only 29 percent of the
cases. This difference persists today.[20]

The second most frequent women's crime, witchcraft, was
not by definition assigned to one sex, but in practice accusations
were almost always against women. Of the thirty-seven cases of
witchcraft heard in the regular sessions of the Massachusetts
Superior Court (the Salem courts were special courts), all but
three were against women. A similar imbalance marked the
Salem cases. These witchcraft prosecutions were heard by three
special courts of oyer and terminer, meeting during the spring
and summer of 1692 at Salem, a time of political and religious
instability and turbulence. The colony was under close scrutiny
in England and was bargaining for its autonomy with little success. In the resulting atmosphere of political tension, women
became scapegoats for general frustration.[21] If "seventeenth-
century witchcraft [had] something to do with the need for
scapegoats in time of intense stress, insecurity, and distraction,
no wonder Increase Mather [the colony's envoy to the king]

returned in the spring of 1692 [from negotiations in London] to find Salem jail full of witches."[22]

It may be argued that these anxieties resulted not in the search for female scapegoats, but for any scapegoat, ending in mass exorcism of evil specters and imps. Against these devils the Salem villagers of Massachusetts first turned to the church. But the ministerial fraternity proved ineffective in banishing the ghosts and devils and only spread the horror stories. Some churchmen were even implicated in the evil spirits' activities. The villagers next begged the aid of the Superior Court. The criminal jurisdiction of the Court of Assistants was suspended owing to the political crisis of 1689, but the same judges who had previously made up the courts of superior jurisdiction agreed to sit on a special court of oyer and terminer to hear the Salem cases. Special courts were common in the colonies and in England, often created to hear a single case or a series of cases. In point of fact, superior courts of law were often asked to hear accusations of witchcraft.[23] From 1630 to 1692 records in New England noted 103 cases of suspected witchcraft; 53 occurred in Massachusetts, and all but one resulted in some official action. The request that a court of oyer and terminer deal with the Salem outbreak was thus not unusual. Before 1692 women predominated among those accused of witchcraft: 44 of the 53 Massachusetts suspects were women. In the Salem crisis 142 of the 201 defendants were women. Though not the only suspects, women were always at greater risk for witchcraft prosecutions than men. The Salem outbreak differed from earlier witchcraft trials not in its focus upon women, but in its high initial conviction and execution rates: 11 of the first 13 tried were convicted and executed. Between 1630 and 1691 only four Massachusetts women had been convicted and executed for witchcraft. Nine women were banished for suspected witchcraft and, more important, because they were Quakers. Twenty-three women were acquitted or dismissed without indictment. The conviction rate for men was about the same, one execution and two other punishments in nine cases. The intensified anxieties in 1692 changed the fate that Salem's accused witches suffered in court, but not women's domination of this category of crime.[24]

Some scholars have linked the witchcraft episode to a more general, deep-seated antipathy toward certain types of women. Nearly all of the suspects at Salem were older women, causing one historian to argue that the displacement of anti-maternal feelings of young girls against parents onto other women was behind the girls' accusations. Other scholars have proposed that a split between the interior of the town—farming Salem—and the more prosperous commercial waterfront exploded in a controversy over the tenure of one minister and fueled the witchcraft trials. Some of the older suspects may have even dabbled in the black arts. The special courts were all male and were perhaps unduly influenced by ministerial animadversions against the sinfulness of women. When the regular sessions of the Superior Court met in Salem in January 1693 to hear the cases of the remaining suspects, the judges did not admit spectral evidence, and the cases against all but three of the still imprisoned fifty-two defendants were dismissed.[25]

Many of these women (in fact, all but one) were reprieved after they confessed to the crime of witchcraft. This series of events, contrary to felony law and usage, further elaborates on women's role as public scapegoats. The court was not lenient to confessed witches because they publicly submitted to the authority of the state.[26] While contriteness of heart through confession was sought from every convicted felon, it did not bring reprieve or pardon. The Superior Court did not pardon women for confessing to infanticide nor men for admitting murder, though confession was urged upon all defendants by the judges. What made the witchcraft cases different? Confession and renunciation of witchcraft showed that the defendant had bowed to the authority of the church, not the court. A defendant's plea for readmission to the church kept the devil at bay and the community secure. Women were harassed by trial and convicted for witchcraft upon flimsy evidence, inadmissible at other times, and then permitted to escape hanging when they recanted (for acts that, in all likelihood, they had never performed) because their reformation proved that the Puritans could overcome the temptations of Satan. The part that women played in the Salem witchcraft outbreak, a part underlined by the court's reprieves, was scripted by religious and social conventions rather than by legal elements of culpability. Witchraft ceased to be a problem after 1693; the offense remained on the books, but no one was charged with it. The devil had evidently decamped for parts unknown.

Like homicide and witchcraft, arson was a more important crime for women than for men—3.6 percent of women's crimes compared to 2.9 percent of men's. Though ostensibly a property crime, it has traditionally been recognized as an aggressive act of revenge. Because it required little skill or physical strength, it was often a weapon of the socially underprivileged: women, racial minorities, and children. Of the total number of arson cases prosecuted in the Superior Court, 23.5 percent were against women. Blacks and Indians accounted for 29.4 percent of those charged, and 26.4 percent were minors. These proportions were higher than these groups' representation for all crimes; women, for example, committed only 19.7 percent of all offenses but 24 percent of all arsons. In 1709 Sabina, "servant or slave" to Richard Saltonstall of Haverhill, "feloniously blew up and destroyed" her master's house "to the danger of his family."[27] In 1681 Maria, another servant woman in Roxbury, pleaded guilty in the Court of Assistants to setting fire to two houses, one of which belonged to her master Joshua Lambe.[28] Hittee, a sixteen-year-old Indian girl from Marblehead, was tried twice—in 1711 for attempted arson and a year later for burning her master's house.[29]

Nonfatal assaults and batteries by women, excluding witchcraft and arson, were rarely prosecuted in the principal courts (although men's assaults and batteries constituted 19 percent of all serious crimes charged against them in the Superior Court, nearly five times greater than the percentage of assaults and batteries by women among women's crimes). The vast majority of these cases were heard in county courts or by individual magistrates. That the Superior Court heard any of them is a reminder of the breadth of its general jurisdiction. The court disposed of misdemeanors at every session, for judges of the high court had commissions that allowed them to hear lesser offenses, both originally and on appeal. If the justices wished, if the king's attorney asked, or if a victim persisted, an assault and battery case could be heard by the Superior Court. From 1673 to 1774, 181 of these cases were tried in the Superior Court, though only eight involved women. All of the latter had special features, which may have induced the court to regard them as serious. In 1759 Sarah Center, a joyner's wife from Billerica, joined two friends, Rebecca Blanchard and Prudence Abbot, both wives of husbandmen, to attack a widowed neighbor, Lydia Hill.[30] None of the women contested the charge. They were fined £8 and required to post sureties for their good behavior until the next term. Perhaps the defendants' concerted action drew the court's attention, which also took notice of women's physical attacks upon government authority. In the generally rebellious decade of the 1760s there were two other cases in which groups of women were accused of beating a deputy sheriff in the course of his duties. Hannah Hall and Elizabeth Shuttleworth, two widows of Upbridge, admitted to charges of striking deputy Ebenezer Waters.[31] Margaret, Mary, and Josiah Gay were all discharged after being found not guilty of routing the deputy sheriff of Suffolk County.[32] Margaret Gay was unique among women defendants for having her occupation listed as "Taylor" with no mention of her marital status.

The next offense that appeared among women's crimes was serious theft. Less than 15 percent of all women's cases were related to stealing, grand larceny, robbery, and burglary. Role theorists have suggested that women usually stole domestic articles—clothes, linen, and housewares—because women were bound to their household role. In Massachusetts women stole clothes and linen in 60.6 percent of their cases. However, household articles, particularly clothing and cloth, were taken in 43 percent of men's thefts as well. In colonial Massachusetts, where manufactured household items and cloth were valuable commodities, criminals of both sexes found them attractive. Inventories of the period show that Massachusetts residents valued their linen as a considerable portion of their personal fortunes. The case records show that women sometimes stole for resale. In 1749 Anne Grafton was charged with three counts of felonious stealing: from William Coffin, A Boston distiller, she took silk and clothes valued at £20; from Samuel Allen, a Boston merchant, she stole £30 worth of clothes; from another merchant, Thomas Jackson, she took

£25 worth of clothes and kitchen goods. Elizabeth (alias Abigail) Howard, a Boston spinster, was twice convicted, in 1743 and 1745, of stealing clothes and linen from Edward Ellis, a Boston physician, and John Bradleigh, a Dorchester housewright, respectively.[33] Not all women stole to resell. Mary Wilkey, her daughter Hannah Minot, and neighbor Phebe White were charged in 1702 with "wickedly and theevishly" stealing an apron, petticoat, and nightdress valued at £4 from merchant Edward Lyde.[34] Other than the gender for which the articles were designed, there is not much difference between these women and Beverly laborer Benjamin Chubb, convicted of stealing a waistcoat and shirt from John Williams's son in 1693, or of the many similar thefts by men in succeeding years.[35]

The last category of serious crime for which women were at all frequently prosecuted was adultery, which comprised 13.4 percent of female crimes. By definition, adultery requires at least an equal number of male perpetrators as female, yet from 1673 to 1774 thirty women and only eight men were charged with adultery. The legal definition of the crime turned on the marital status of the woman, not the man, but each offense required two offenders. In point of fact, the criminal burden seemed to rest with the woman. Sexual morality was a question of social control in Massachusetts as in other societies. One way to insure the safety of the patriarchal family structure was to control female sexual promiscuity. In theory this could be applied to men as well, but it rarely was.[36]

Despite the rigors of Puritan domestic precepts, every county court in the Bay Colony was plagued with cases of fornication. The records for Plymouth County, conveniently and thoroughly edited by David Konig, show a three-to-one ratio of females to males accused of fornication in the colonial period.[37] When one turns to the church records for the years 1620–1769, relying on the work of Emil Oberholtzer, one finds an even greater disproportion between the numbers of women and men accused.[38] Accusations are not facts, although the vast preponderance of these accusations resulted in some form of punishment—a way of keeping order (versus determining guilt) familiar to modern students of criminal justice.

Contemporary authorities may have thought that adultery by a woman had more serious consequences than adultery by a man, since if the woman became pregnant, the result would be lasting embarrassment and an economic threat to legitimate heirs. The fact of pregnancy itself might also make it easier to convict adulterous women than adulterous men.

The discrepancy in indictments also applies to the other sexual morality crimes common to both sexes. Though only a minor component of crimes for both men and women, incest/buggery/bigamy was a greater percentage of women's cases than men's (2.7 percent versus 1.5 percent). Six of the twenty cases (30 percent) of crimes in this category were prosecuted against women, though women accounted for only 19.7 percent of all serious crimes.

The Defendants

Were felonies committed by a "dangerous class" of women: repeaters, conspirators, and perpetually violent members of an underclass? Hardly. The record shows about as much diversity in characteristics of defendants as in their offenses.

The first characteristic of a female suspect to be noted in the indictment, and in many ways the most important, was marital status. Marriage was the norm for women in colonial Massachusetts, and almost all women (the ratio approaches 90 percent) eventually married. An unmarried woman was either out-of-step with her peers or in transition from youth to adulthood. These were perceived by ministers and lawmakers as dangerous stages of life, times of vulnerability. Information on the marital status of female defendants is available for over 90 percent of those charged with serious crimes in the high courts of Massachusetts. Table 3 shows that almost half of the female defendants (105 of 224, or 46.9 percent) were single, and that married women comprised more than one-third of all accused women (83 of 224, or 37.1 percent).

Serious sexual offenses were overwhelmingly committed by married women, largely because the most frequent charge in this category (adultery) was by definition committed by married or espoused women. Sophisticated offenses against property, particularly counterfeiting and passing of counter-

TABLE 3. Marital Status of Women Accused of Serious
Crimes in Massachusetts, 1673–1774

Marital Status	Number	Percentage
Single	105	46.9
Married	83	37.1
Widow	15	6.7
Separated	1	0.4
Unknown	20	8.9
Total	224	100.0

feit paper, were committed almost evenly by single, married, and widowed women. Stealing, like homicide, was usually a crime of single, lower-class women, though a significant proportion of those accused (30 percent) were married. A cross-tabulation enables us to explore these connections more closely (see Appendix 1, Table A1.1).

Homicide was committed primarily by single women, 72 percent of the total. This is consistent with the fact that the primary victims of women's murderous aggression were their own bastard infants. Examples are both plentiful and tragically repetitive. Ester Rogers was accused of killing her female bastard in Newbury in 1701.[39] Sarah Goldthwaite, a single woman of Lynn, was indicted for the murder of her male bastard in 1772.[40] Though the majority of women accused of homicide were single, eighteen of seventy-five were married. Mary Flood, the wife of Henry, was accused of killing her youngest daughter, age thirteen weeks, in Boston in 1686.[41] The only case in which an indicted woman was separated from her husband was that of Sarah Smith. At the time of the crime, in 1698, Smith's husband was a captive of the Indians, leaving Sarah alone in the frontier town of Deerfield. Sarah conceived a child in an adulterous union and then "strangled, smothered and neglected" her newborn daughter, in the words of the indictment, "with intent to conceal her lewdness."[42]

Some portion of the concentration of serious women's crimes in the area of sexual deviance may be ascribed to the difference between the official mores of the community and the customary license allowed women in their own "small

world." The notion that women lived in two worlds, one public that was governed by men, and largely closed to women's
aspirations, and the other that was private, domestic, and directed by a hierarchy of male figures, is appealing to social
historians. It opens a wealth of insights into the perceptions of
ordinary women, alternative insights to those one might erro-
neously derive from reliance upon the official pronouncements of lawgivers, ministers, and heads of families. That the
rules of conduct in the private world of growing girls were
wholly different from those demanded by authorities is indicated by the fact that premarital fornication was condemned
harshly in the public world, but, if the records of the courts of
general sessions are any indication, widely practiced by young
women. Did such divergence lead to more serious crimes?[43]

Although I do not subscribe to the theory that lesser offenses are a prelude to more serious crimes (a theory cur-
rently applied to drug abuse, juvenile delinquency, and sexual
promiscuity by some modern writers), early modern Massachusetts authorities evidently accepted this premise. To
judge from the "gallows sermons" of leading Puritan ministers
throughout the period of this study, wicked women left a trail
of increasingly serious crimes on their way to the noose. Certainly the accounts in the sermons of the careers of the few
women actually executed seem to bear out this thesis. However, close reading of these sermons shows not a pattern of
prior arrests and investigations, but a pattern of successfully
concealed crimes. It was the concealment, not the public record of crime, that the ministers stressed in their admonitions
against lesser offenses. In fact, there was very little recidivism
in the criminal record of the highest courts. Only 18 of 224
women were accused of more than one serious crime at any
time in their adult lives, a mere 8.5 percent of all women
brought to the principal criminal courts. Recidivism was not
much higher when one includes the prior presentments of
these women in their county courts. A few had run into
trouble before, but most had not.[44] Within Eli Faber's "co-
hort," earlier in the century, there was a 42.2 percent repeater
rate.[45] Ten recidivists in the high court were tried for property offenses, though only one for counterfeiting or other

sophisticated property crimes. This alone can hardly prove that such women belonged to criminal gangs in a subculture of thieves. Eighteenth-century Anglo-American cities and rural areas had such gangs, but also had destitute and hungry women who might steal to survive. One must also remember that execution of offenders reduces recidivism—but, as Chapter 5 demonstrates, few women were actually hanged.

Some scholars have proposed that preindustrial, nonurban societies regard newcomers (particularly of low status) or unattached strangers as suspicious, and thus the residence of offenders might have been a significant factor in indictments. The data disprove that hypothesis, at least when applied to seventeenth- and eighteenth-century Massachusetts women (see Appendix 1, Table A1.2). Only 5.3 percent of the 224 defendants were strangers to the jurors. Most of the defendants were residents of a village or town in the county, though not the town in which the court sat. This fact probably reflects Massachusetts demography: most people did not live in county seats but in the surrounding area. Those who did live in the county seat, nearly one-third, might be slightly overrepresented in court cases because they were easier to identify and prosecute.

Ethnic/racial factors did carry some weight in criminal indictments and committals (see Appendix 1, Table A1.3). Nearly 84 percent of women defendants were white Englishwomen (or at least had English names). Only 8 percent were black or mulatto women (a fact noted in the record), and 5.4 percent were Indian (also noted in the record), but in proportion to their numbers blacks and mulattos were slightly overrepresented among those accused of serious crimes. Blacks and mulattos (whose crimes and characteristics are grouped together here) were never more than 2 or 3 percent of the Massachusetts population, but female blacks and mulattos were three times as frequently indicted for crimes as white women.[46] Indians comprised perhaps as much as 7 percent of the colony's populace, and female Indians were, in theory, proportionally represented among the defendants.[47] Most of the Indians lived in praying towns—enclaves within the settlements. The few who lived among the whites, like the blacks, were overrepresented in the high courts' dock.

There was a pattern in the prosecution of the three primary ethnic groups—white, black, and Indian—and the types of crimes for which each racial group as indicted varied strikingly (See Appendix 1 Table A1.4). Certain crimes were uniquely linked to whites: sophisticated property offenses and sexual/morality charges. Counterfeiting and uttering (passing counterfeit money) were not crimes in which women participated generally (only 5 percent of the total number of crimes for which they were indicted). These offenses required skill and economic involvement, which women seldom had. Minority females were even less likely to have such opportunities: accessibility to currency would be required, and blacks and Indians were rarely allowed to handle money. In the "other property" category, 14 percent of those indicted for simple thefts belonged to racial minorities. Also included in this category were arsons, which were associated then as now with disadvantaged social groups. Indifference to the sexual behavior of minorities by white male authorities seems an obvious answer to the lack of minority defendants in the sex/morals crime category. Adultery and incest among Indians and blacks were no threat to the social order of whites.

On the other hand, the killing of bastard children was not a sex offense, and minority women were prosecuted for murdering their children. Of the twenty-one minority defendants accused of homicide, eighteen were charged with infanticide.

Blacks and Indians were strongly represented in the total number of homicides: 15.6 percent of all homicides were charged against the former, and 11.7 percent to the latter. Blacks and Indians living among the whites were servants, often running afoul of the bastardy laws and thereby motivated to do away with unwanted bastard newborns.

Minority groups might, in fact, be particularly called to task for the violent breach of fundamental social behavior. Judges and juries at the high court most often saw blacks and Indians in murder and manslaughter cases, for two-thirds of serious black crime and three-fourths of serious Indian crime were homicides. The white majority treated these groups with repressive measures and may have reacted strongly to suspicions of violence among racial minorities.[48]

The Victims

The systematic study of the victims of crimes—victimology—is still in its infancy, but the impact of the victims' characteristics upon grand juries in women's cases should not be ignored (see Appendix 1, Table A1.5). The majority of women's victims for whom we know age—54.4 percent—were adults. Age seems to be strongly related to type of crime. Sixty-three of the sixty-seven children who suffered at the hands of women were victims of homicide. This is consistent with what we know about women and infanticide indictments in colonial Massachusetts.[49] Adult victims comprised only 13.8 percent of female homicide cases, 23.8 percent of other personal offenses, and 62.5 percent of property crimes. Women killed children and stole from adults. Women's limited social role partially explains their attacks against children: children were their most accessible and vulnerable outlet. Likewise, adults were the owners of property and thus the victims of property crimes. There is no strong pattern for convictions related to age of victim. Sixty percent or more of the women accused of killing children of every age were acquitted. The courts were a little more severe toward women who killed adults: convictions and acquittals were nearly equally split, with a slight leaning toward acquittals.

The relationship of the victim to the accused also affected indictments. (See Appendix 1, Table A1.6). Not surprisingly, the familial relationship most strongly represented among women's victims was that of mother-child. A small percentage of victims were the masters of the accused (servants accounted for 18 percent of the women indicted). Only one spouse was a victim of serious female crime—Margaret Knodle's husband. Women were never indicted for killing their husbands, though 20 percent of men's homicide cases involved husbands killing wives. The largest category of relationship was that of no familial relationship at all. These nonrelated victims were divided by crime type between property offenses (48.5 percent) and other personal charges (39.8 percent). Homicides of nonfamily members account for a mere 11.8 percent of indictments. There is no strong correlation between the relationship of the accused to the victim and the outcome of the trial.

Of the 137 victims of female crime whose gender is known, 52.6 percent were males. Patterns emerge in this gender division according to the type of crime (see Appendix 1, Table A1.7). Dividing crimes into categories and comparing them to the gender of victim reveals that the largest segment of female victims appear in the category "other personal." These females were, for the most part (twenty-two of twenty-eight), the victims of the aberrant witchcraft accusations. When these victims are removed from the total number of female victims, the proportion of all victims represented by males rises almost eleven percentage points. Male victims, on the other hand, were almost evenly divided between property crimes and homicide. It is easy to explain the high percentage of male victims of females' property crimes. Men were the legal owners of all property in the colony except that controlled by *femes sole* and widows. Men were named as victims when goods were stolen from houses, stores, homes, and ships, even when the items were women's apparel, linen, and personal effects.[50] Male victims of homicide were almost invariably children. For unmarried mothers, perhaps frightened and certainly abandoned by their male lovers, the sex of the newborn child might have connected the latter to the absent father. The mother's resentment and agression toward the source of her predicament might have led to an attack upon offspring of the same gender. This is highly speculative, but it might explain the predominance of males in the sex of murdered bastard infants.[51]

Women's and Men's Crimes Compared

From the study of the distribution of crime by defendants' gender and the types of victims men and women selected, a tentative conclusion emerges: the two sexes did not commit the various types of serious crime in similar proportion. Table 4 illustrates these differences.

The most striking difference between the indictments of females and males for felony is in murder and manslaughter. Homicide represented less than one-fifth of male prosecutions but was over one-third of all criminal indictments against

60

TABLE 4. Females and Males Accused of Serious Crimes in Massachusetts, 1673–1774

Crime	Male		Female		Total	
	Number	Percentage[a]	Number	Percentage[b]	Number	Percentage
Murder/manslaughter	166	18.2	77	34.4	243	21.4
Witchcraft	2	0.2	34	15.2	36	3.2
Adultery	8	0.9	30	13.4	38	3.3
Incest/buggery/bigamy	14	1.5	6	2.7	20	1.8
Arson	26	2.9	8	3.6	34	3.0
Burglary/felonious stealing/ breaking and entering	268	29.4	33	14.7	301	26.5
Counterfeit/uttering/ forgery	174	19.1	11	4.9	185	16.3
Assault/rape	173	19.0	8	3.6	181	15.9
Other, personal	16	1.8	8	3.6	24	2.1
Other, property	36	3.9	9	4.0	45	4.0
Other, public	29	3.2	0	0.0	29	2.6
Total	912	100.1[c]	224	100.1[c]	1,136	100.1[c]

Note. Of the 1,136 individuals accused of serious crimes, males comprised 80.3 percent of the total; females, 19.7 percent.
[a]The percentage is of the total number of males accused.
[b]The percentage is of the total number of females accused.
[c]Percentages are greater than 100 due to rounding.

women. The discrepancies in witchcraft and adultery accusations have already been discussed. Other discrepancies are clear in the theft and counterfeiting categories. As a percentage of all-male crimes, burglary/felonious stealing/breaking and entering was twice as frequent for men as for women, and counterfeiting/uttering/forgery was nearly four times as frequent among male crimes as female. Whereas women were more involved as a group in violent crimes that resulted in the death of the victim, men were considerably more prone to assaults that stopped short of fatality—nearly five times the percentage of all crimes for women.

These discrepancies can be summarized by collapsing the crimes into two major categories: personal crime and property crime, as in Table 5. There is a strong association between sex and crime type: women primarily committed crimes against persons; men were most often involved in crimes against property.

TABLE 5. Personal and Property Crimes, by Females and Males, in Massachusetts, 1673–1774

Crimes	Female		Male	
	Number	Percentage	Number	Percentage
Against persons	127	67.6	357	41.5
Against property	61	32.4	504	58.5
Total	188		861	

Note. $Q = -.49$. Males committed 82.1 percent of the total number of crimes; females, 17.9 percent.

Women's Crimes over Time

The opportunities for women to commit crimes changed as the Bay Colony moved from a semi-isolated, rural, agricultural community to an outpost of imperial commercialism. The rise of modern societies is a subject of much controversy in the historical profession today, but no one doubts the transformation that occurred in the economic life of Massachusetts between 1650 and 1750.[52] Two phenomena that became superimposed upon each other redirected women's criminal activity. The first was a vast change in the role of the individual in society. This modernization of human relationships had been long in coming—indeed, it had hardly begun by 1700—but its presence was felt everywhere. The increasing complexity in ordinary life, particularly in Boston, manifested itself in the secular, materialistic, and self-determining spirit anathema to Puritans of Cotton Mather's generation. The rapid diversification of economic activity, the rage for speculation and expansion, and a burst of extra-premarital sexual activity were all bound up in this shift from communitarian to individualistic values.[53] The second trend involved land, as many Massachusetts towns reached the limits of their available land. A period of uncertain prices, growing fixity of economic classes, and labor unrest set in across the entire Atlantic seaboard.[54] Michael Hindus argues that crime in America responded to the growth of a commercial economy. "The incidence, as well as relative importance, of crimes against property [vis-à-vis crimes against the person] should increase as social stratification becomes more pronounced and as a commercial economy replaces subsistence agriculture."[55] The growth of theft, particularly sophisticated theft, in urban and commercial centers opened new opportunities for crime to women. Whether these are referred to as "white-collar crimes," as Hindus does—following the concept originated by Edwin Sutherland—or "theft-by-trick," as Eric Monkkonen does, such crimes include forgery, counterfeiting, and fraud. (Monkkonen adds receiving stolen goods to the category; I assign it to property crime.) Figure 1 shows both the increase in number of property crimes committed by women in Massachusetts between the 1670s and 1774 and also how these crimes became a greater percentage of all crimes committed by women. The figures for the 1770s only include the years 1770–74 and thus represent perhaps only half of the real crimes prosecuted in that decade. There apparently was a steady increase in absolute numbers of crimes in the eighteenth century, led by property crimes, and by the 1740s these crimes had become a more important part of women's total crimes than offenses against the person.

Absolute numbers can be deceiving. Although the number of personal and property offenses by women seem to have increased during the century, the population in Massachusetts

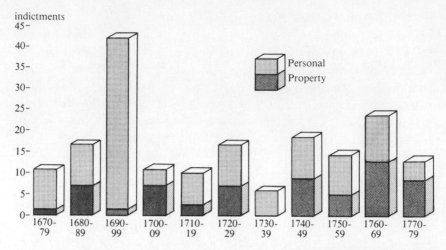

FIGURE 1. Personal and Property Crimes Committed by Females, by Decade, 1670s–1774

increased as well. Did the rise in female crime keep pace with the steady growth of population? The standard way of dealing with this question is to calculate the ratio of crimes to the population of adult females at risk to commit crimes,[56] as in Figure 2.

Sex and morals offenses, which had played a greater role in women's offenses than men's, ceased to be a central concern of the courts as the eighteenth century progressed. David H. Flaherty has argued that the courts came to believe that law enforcement and the imposition of moral standards were not the same, at least in matters of private sexual conduct.[57] The disappearance of fornication cases from the dockets of the high courts may well be evidence of such a philosophical shift. Local courts, however, continued to prosecute bastardy and fornication cases and ministers and other moral authorities continued to inveigh against sexual irregularity.[58]

If the alteration in attitudes about sex removed many of the lesser offenses from the high court, such attitudes did not change the sober view that justices took of serious morals offenses. After a sharp drop, especially in fornication cases, the rate of sexual offenses became quite stable. Serious sexual offenses, including adultery, while no longer treated as felo-

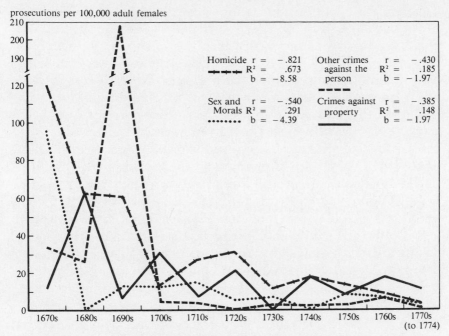

prosecutions per 100,000 adult females

Homicide	r =	−.821	Other crimes	r =	−.430
	R² =	.673	against the	R² =	.185
	b =	−8.58	person	b =	−1.97
Sex and	r =	−.540	Crimes against	r =	−.385
Morals	R² =	.291	property	R² =	.148
	b =	−4.39		b =	−1.97

FIGURE 2. Adult Female Prosecution Rates of Major Crimes in
Massachusetts, 1673–1774

nies, were nevertheless important enough to be heard by the
Superior Court. As in other cases, the court had redefined
itself as a hearer of serious crimes, and these offenses by
women remained serious. Simple fornication, which may have
in fact been growing (the rate of premarital pregnancy leaped
upward), did not threaten family and affront religion; adultery did.

It is clear from Figure 2 that a smaller and smaller proportion of women out of the total of adult women in the
population were committing homicide and personal crimes.
This decline was led by the rapid diminution of fatal personal
crimes. Female rates for homicide per 100,000 population declined by 8.56 cases per decade between 1673 and 1774. Men's
homicide rates declined by 11.5 cases per decade during this
period, though the decline was less tied to the time factor than
it was for women (R^2 = .450 for men vs. R^2 = .673 for
women).[59] The decline in crimes of violence generally has
been noted by both Hindus and Monkkonen. Women's homi-

cide rates may have declined more rapidly than men's (Figure 3) because social attitudes, particularly toward sex, were changing rapidly. The decline in the severity of punishment for bastardy may have lessened social stigma and thereby removed a major motive for murdering bastard children.

The variation over time of rates of property crimes was less uniform than those of personal crimes, and the overall pattern was slightly U-shaped. Even without the troughs for rates of crimes against property in the 1710s, 1730s, and 1750s, the overall rate of property crime would have generally declined between 1673 and 1774 by almost two cases per decade. Though the rate appears to fall steeply when these drops are included, the rates actually remained stable between 1730 and 1774. Indeed, for the last two decades, the rates slightly, though not significantly, increased. The eighteenth century thus saw a slowly changing pattern of relationship between personal and property crimes. Until 1700 crimes against property by women varied inversely with their crimes

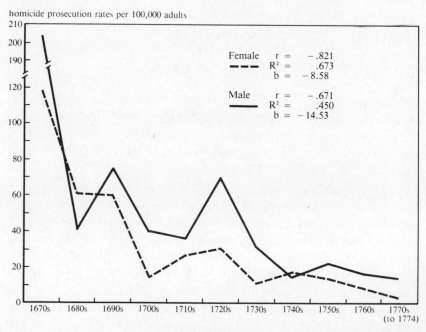

FIGURE 3. Adult Male and Female Homicide Prosecution Rates in Massachusetts, 1673–1774

against persons. In the 1720s through the 1750s the two crime types varied almost in tandem. In the 1760s female property crimes exceeded all other crimes for the first time.

There is some evidence that all societies, including Puritan New England, have a more or less stable level of crime.[60] If such is the case, prosecution for offenses against property and against the person may be inversely related. But such a homeopathic system will break apart when new social and economic forces are introduced, and society's structure is altered. These new forces change the level and distribution of crimes. The years between 1730 and 1750 were such a time in Massachusetts. The mixture of rising expectations and diminishing economic opportunities for the very poor had a direct effect on crime rates. Property crimes by both men and women increased (as Hindus's theory predicts). By the 1760s the rise in property crimes had first outstripped the comparatively slower growth of personal offenses and then leveled off, while the rate of crimes against persons declined.

But the effects of changing social and economic conditions were not felt in the same way by potential female and male criminals. This is clear from Table 6, which shows a decline in female participation in serious crimes ($R^2 = .465$),

TABLE 6. Females as a Percentage of the Total Number of Defendants for Serious Crime in Massachusetts, 1673–1774

Decade	Percentage
1670s	32.56
1680s	38.64
1690s	60.29[a]
1700s	19.64
1710s	10.42
1720s	12.59
1730s	8.21
1740s	20.21
1750s	13.04
1760s	11.76
1770s	9.46

[a]This does not include the special courts of oyer and terminer held in Salem.

with a reduction of three and one-third percentage points each decade. This may be attributed to fewer female crimes per adult females, or to a second, more complicated mechanism: the increasing unwillingness of the authorities to prosecute females for serious crimes.

Is the latter the case? If so, female crime in colonial Massachusetts presents a more complex pattern than changing distributions and rates over time. From the evidence in chapters 1 and 2, we may assert that the highest courts gradually found fornication less threatening and so cases of this type were relegated to the lower courts. Thus the rates of sex and morals crimes seen by the Superior Court judges would automatically decline. The small but steady level of more serious sexual offenses adjudicated by the high court would then suggest the undiminished threat that gross perversion had for the society as a whole. The fall of crimes against persons by women defendants was as marked as the shift in handling sexual offenses. The two largest categories of serious female personal crimes were homicide and witchcraft, both of which can be expressions of frustration and relative impotence of women; witchcraft disappeared as a criminal charge in the eighteenth century. Chapter 4 pursues this thesis, that crime rates were substantially determined by the concerns of the men who stood in judgment over women.

NOTES

1. The best recent account of the lesser offenses heard in the county court is Paul Donald Marsella's "Criminal Cases at the Essex County, Massachusetts, Court of General Sessions, 1700–1785" (Ph.D. diss., University of New Hampshire, 1982), but see also David H. Flaherty, "Crime and Social Control in Provincial Massachusetts," *Historical Journal* 24 (1981), 341; Lyle Koehler, *A Search for Power: The "Weaker Sex" in Seventeenth-Century New England* (Urbana, Ill., 1980), 193; and William Nelson, *Dispute and Conflict Resolution in Plymouth County, 1725–1825* (Chapel Hill, N.C., 1981), 159n63.

2. Nelson, *Dispute and Conflict*, 26–44.

3. Joseph H. Smith, ed., *The Pynchon Court Record* (Cambridge, Mass., 1961).

4. For example, J. M. Beattie, "Towards a Study of Crime in 18th-Century England: A Note on Indictments," in *The Triumph of Culture: Eighteenth-Century Perspectives*, Paul Fritz and David Williams ed. (Toronto, 1972), 314.

5. While petty crimes are unreported 78 percent of the time today, serious crimes like burglary are reported 70 percent of the time. See J. Ernst Eck and Lucius J. Riccio, "Relationship between Reported Crime Rates and Victimization Survey Results," *Journal of Criminal Justice* 7 (Winter 1979), 295.

6. David T. Konig, *Law and Society in Puritan Massachusetts: Essex County, 1629–1692* (Chapel Hill, N.C., 1979), 187, and Nelson, *Dispute and Conflict,* 22–26, argue that Massachusetts settlers had confidence in the courts to settle personal disputes.

7. Michael Weisser, *Crime and Punishment in Early Modern Europe* (Atlantic Highlands, N.J., 1979), 80, 84; J. M. Beattie, "Crime and the Courts in Surrey, 1736–1753," in J. S. Cockburn, ed., *Crime in England, 1550–1800* (London, 1977), 158.

8. See, for example, Dale Hoffman-Bustamente, "The Nature of Female Criminality," *Issues in Criminology* 8 (Fall 1973), 121–31, and Carol Smart, *Women, Crime and Criminology: A Feminist Critique* (London, 1976), 66–70.

9. Particularly on homicide, see Marvin Wolfgang, *Patterns of Criminal Homicide* (Philadelphia, 1958), 207, and Wolfgang, "Husband-Wife Homicides," *Journal of Social Therapy* 2 (1956), 263–71. On female aggressive crime generally, see David J. Pittman and William Handy, "Patterns in Criminal Aggravated Assault," in *Crime in America,* ed. Bruce J. Cohen, 2d ed. (Itasca, Ill., 1977), 115, 118, 119–20.

10. Peter C. Hoffer and N. E. H. Hull, *Murdering Mothers: Infanticide in England and New England, 1558–1803* (New York, 1981), ch. 2. Mather's maid is discussed by Samuel Sewall in a May 11, 1686, diary entry; see *Diary of Samuel Sewall,* ed. M. Halsey Thomas (New York, 1972), 1:110.

11. The two cases are Phillis of Boston, SCJ 1750–51, 180 (Feb. 19, 1751), and Phillis of Charlestown, SCJ 1755–56, 123–24 (Aug. 1, 1755).

12. Ford's case, SCJ 1: 129–30 (Oct. 30, 1694).

13. Patience's case, SCJ 1733–36, 228 (June 18, 1735).

14. Eams's case, SCJ 1769, 221 (Nov. 7–15, 1769).

15. Otto Pollak, *The Criminality of Women* (Philadelphia, 1950), 23–24.

16. McNeal's case, SCJ 1760–62, 321–22 (Feb. 16, 1762).

17. Remington's case, SCJ 1715–21, 256 (Dec. 1718).

18. Throop's case, SCJ 1715–21, 319 (Sept. 13, 1720).

19. Some cases of suspicious death, called "homicides" in the records, were heard in the county courts. These could not be punished as felonious killings, for the county courts did not have the power of life and limb. While such cases might have been murders, county courts regarded them as excusable homicides (self-defense or a killing committed while aiding in the capture of a felon) or as accidental deaths by "misadventure," which occurred while the suspect was "in the king's peace." Such cases might come to the county courts because of the convenience of their holdings, because an action for civil damages was involved, or perhaps because an individual incarcerated for suspicion of a felony homicide obtained counsel to plead his cause to the local court. Such cases, if the king's attorney decided to prosecute for the murder, eventually went to the Superior Court when it sat in the county. On this point, see William Nelson, "Emerging Notions of Mod-

ern Criminal Law in the Revolutionary Era: An Historical Perspective," *New York University Law Review* 2 (May 1967), 450–82. A report of murder could always be brought to the county court in a suit for libel; see, for example, in *Kent vs. Smith*, Aug. 8, 1672, in *Records of the Suffolk County Court, 1671–1680*, Publications of the Colonial Society of Massachusetts (Boston, 1933), 29:128.

20. Marvin Wolfgang, "A Sociological Analysis of Criminal Homicide," *Federal Probation* 25 (Mar. 1961), 52–53; Alex D. Pokorny, "A Comparison of Homicide in Two Cities," *Journal of Criminal Law, Criminology and Police Science* 56 (1965).

21. Hoffer and Hull, *Murdering Mothers,* 56–57.

22. David S. Lovejoy, *The Glorious Revolution in America* (New York, 1972), 353.

23. But for a contrary view, see Konig, *Law and Society,* 169–71.

24. Data are from Koehler, *Search for Power,* 474–91. See also John Putnam Demos, *Entertaining Satan: Witchcraft and the Culture of Early New England* (New York, 1983), 55–94.

25. Demos, "Underlying Themes in the Witchcraft of 17th-Century New England," *American Historical Review* 75 (1970), 1311–26; Paul Boyer and Stephen Nissenbaum, *Salem Possessed* (Cambridge, Mass., 1975), passim; Marion L. Starkey, *The Devil in Massachusetts* (New York, 1949), 48; Chadwick Hansen, *Witchcraft at Salem* (New York, 1969), 122–23, 126–27, 137, 204–5.

26. Konig, *Law and Society,* 175.

27. Sabina's case SCJ 3:238 (May 4, 1709).

28. Maria's case, *Court of Assistants,* 1: 359 (1681).

29. Hittee's case, SCJ 3: 270 (Mar. 25, 1712).

30. Center's case, SCJ 1757–59, 654–55 (Aug. 7, 1759).

31. Hall's case, SCJ 1764–65, 274 (Sept. 17, 1765).

32. Gay's case, SCJ 1763–64, 132 (Aug. 16, 1763).

33. Grafton's case, SCJ 1747–50, 275 (Aug. 15, 1749); Elizabeth Howard's case, SCJ 1743–47, 33 (Aug. 16, 1743); Abigail Howard's case, SCJ 1743–47, 160 (Mar. 7, 1745). If one were to add petty theft, which was handled at the local or county court level, to the totals, the ratio of female to male participation in crimes against property would increase sharply. According to colonial New York and Canadian court records, and later Massachusetts's state incarceration records, in proportion to men, women took part in far more petty thefts than they did in robberies and burglaries. When one confines oneself to serious crimes, as here, women return to their minor role. See, for comparisons, Douglass Greenberg, *Crimes and Law Enforcement in the Colony of New York, 1691–1776* (Ithaca, N.Y., 1976), 50–51; Andre Lachance, "Women and Crime in Canada in the Early Eighteenth Century, 1712–1759," in *Crime and Criminal Justice in Europe and Canada,* ed. Louis A. Knafla (Waterloo, 1981), 162–63. For a contrary view, see the results for serious crimes as given in Michael Stephen Hindus, *Prison and Plantation: Crime, Justice, and Authority in Massachusetts and South Carolina, 1767–1878* (Chapel Hill, N.C., 1980), 82.

34. Wilkey's case, SCJ 3: 69 (May 5, 1702).

35. Chubb's case, SCJ 1: 112 (May 15, 1694).

36. Nancy F. Cott, "Divorce and the Changing Status of Women in Eighteenth-Century Massachusetts," *William and Mary Quarterly*, 3d ser., 33 (1976), 586–614, traces one such control mechanism.

37. David T. Konig, ed., *Plymouth [County] Court Records, 1683–1820* (Wilmington, Del., 1978), vols. 2 and 3, passim.

38. Emil Oberholtzer, Jr., *Delinquent Saints* (New York, 1956), 255.

39. Rogers's case, SCJ 3:49 (July 15, 1701); see also *Diary of Sewall*, 1:451.

40. Goldthwaite's case, SCJ 1772, 98–99 (June 20, 1772).

41. Flood's case, *Court of Assistants*, 1:295 (Mar. 3, 1686); *Suffolk Co. Court Records*, 29:82–85, 99.

42. Smith's case, SCJ 2:193–94 (Aug. 18, 1698); *Suffolk Co. Court Records*, 41:74–75. On Smith, see also Cotton Mather, *Pillars of Salt* (Boston, 1699), 3ff.

43. On crime and the private world of women, see Eldon R. Turney, "Gender, Abortion, and Testimony: A Textual Look at the Martin Case, Middlesex County, Massachusetts, 1681–1683," ms. in my possession, cited by permission.

44. Rates of recidivism in colonial Massachusetts were very low compared with modern rates. The latter vary, according to the formula used to compute such rates, from a low of 30 percent to a high of 70 percent; see Sue Titus Reid, *Crime and Criminology*, 2d ed. (New York, 1979), 755–60.

45. Of the seven women from Plymouth accused of serious crimes, for example, none had prior prosecutions in the general session of the Plymouth county court. Eli Faber, "Puritan Criminals: The Economic, Social, and Intellectual Background to Crime in 17th-Century Massachusetts," *Perspectives in American History* 11 (1978), 133, found that 42.2 percent of the families that came into court had at least one repeater. The rate of recidivism of defendants tried in the lower courts of New York Colony has been computed as 16 percent, see Greenberg, *Crime and Law Enforcement in the Colony of New York*, 211. In the county of Richmond, Virginia, the rate of recidivism of all defendants was 19 percent; see Peter C. Hoffer and William B. Scott, *Criminal Trials in Colonial Virginia: The Richmond County Record, 1711–1754*, vol. 10 of American Legal Records Series (Athens, Ga., 1984), lxvi.

46. Robert V. Wells, *The Population of the British Colonies in America before 1776: A Survey of Census Data* (Princeton, N.J., 1975), 81.

47. Ibid., 81.

48. By 1705 "non-whites were openly and obviously equated with *chattel*." Curfews and prejudicial regulations were applied to servants and free blacks as well as slaves; see A. Leon Higginbotham, Jr., *In the Matter of Color: Race and the American Legal Process, the Colonial Period* (New York, 1978), 78–79.

49. Today "women usually kill their husbands, lovers, or children," but only the last part of this generalization was true in colonial Massachusetts. See Jane Totman, *The Murderess: A Psychosocial Study of Criminal Homicide* (San Francisco, 1978), 3.

50. Richard B. Morris, *Studies in the History of American Law*, 2d ed. (New York, 1958), 126–200.

51. Joseph C. Rhinegold, *The Fear of Being a Woman* (New York, 1964), 143ff.

52. The general trend toward a complex, secular, materialistic, voluntary, and self-determining society in the West was the broad phenomenon into which the Massachusetts case fit; see Richard M. Brown, *Modernization: The Transformation of American Life, 1600–1865* (New York, 1976), 3–22. On the colony itself, see Ronald P. Dufour, "Modernization in Colonial Massachusetts, 1630–1763" (Ph.D. diss., College of William and Mary, 1982).

53. Richard Hofstadter, *America at 1750: A Social Portrait* (New York, 1973), 148, 150; James A. Henretta, *The Evolution of American Society, 1700–1815* (Lexington, Mass., 1973), 103.

54. Gary B. Nash, *The Urban Crucible: Social Change, Political Consciousness, and the Origins of the American Revolution* (Cambridge, Mass., 1979), 61ff.

55. Michael Hindus, "The Social Context of Crime in Massachusetts and South Carolina, 1760–1873: Theoretical and Quantitative Perspectives," *Newberry Papers in Family and Community History.* (Sept. 1976), #75-3, 5; see also Eric H. Monkkonen, *The Dangerous Class: Crime and Poverty in Columbus, Ohio, 1860–1885* (Cambridge, Mass., 1975), 26–27.

56. Using the total population estimates for each decade, one can arrive at a tentative estimate of the adult female population. First, the sex ratio for the period 1670 to 1700 was slightly greater than one man to one woman, as is true in all frontier communities. By the 1700s this had changed to a relatively stable ratio of 1.05 males per females. Over the entire period 1670 to 1774, the percentage of children in the population probably varied between 40 percent and 50 percent of the total population. Thus, for the years before 1700 total population was multiplied by (.60) for adults × (.40) for females = .24. For the period after 1700, the multiplier was .30. The number of criminal indictments recorded for the decade was divided by ten and then divided again by the estimated adult female population for the average year in the decade. The resulting crime rate was then multiplied by a constant of 100,000 to standardize the figures and so permit comparison of rates from areas and periods with different populations. Decadal population figures were drawn from U.S. Bureau of the Census, *A Century of Population Growth* (Washington, D.C., 1909), "Colonial Population," 9–10. Sex ratios and age structure were taken from Wells, *Population of the British Colonies before 1776*, 83–85.

57. David H. Flaherty, "Law and the Enforcement of Morals in Early America," *Perspectives on American History* 5 (1971), 250.

58. William E. Nelson, *Americanization of the Common Law: The Impact of Legal Change, 1760–1830* (Cambridge, Mass., 1975), 37–38.

59. R^2 = .450 for men, not as strong as R^2 = .673 for women, showing the explanatory power that passing time alone had upon criminal activity.

60. Kai T. Erikson, *Wayward Puritans: A Study in the Sociology of Deviance* (New York, 1966), 174, and Hindus, "Social Context of Crime," 8–9.

72

CHAPTER FOUR

WOMEN AND FELONY PROCEDURE
FROM REPORT TO TRIAL

Chapter 3 reveals a picture of diverse criminality imputed to women, of crimes associated with measurable external forces similar to those that induced men to steal and defraud. There is also a noticeable difference between the modal crimes, that is, the typical serious offenses supposedly committed by men and women. But are these imputations and suppositions of criminality warranted? Did women actually commit the crimes of which they stood accused? The question has two parts. First, how did women come to be accused of crime? Given the invidious distinctions that preachers made about sinful women and that lawgivers laid down about deviant women, one must seek reassurance that magistrates and constables were not predisposed to seek out and punish women for crimes that women did not commit. One does not have to ascribe a raving misogyny to these men, merely a credulity, a willingness to believe without much proof, that certain kinds of women were likely to commit certain crimes; that women's nature alone provided a motive, where none could be established from testimony; and that women's weaknesses could be a driving force to commit a crime so obvious that no evidence of opportunity need be offered. The answer to the second question entails analysis of verdicts in women's cases. We will tackle it in Chapter 5.

Even for the earliest courts of the colony, when Puritanism held sway, institutional bias is hard to prove.[1] There was no attempt to provide separate courts for women or to introduce separate procedures for handling them. As the bench became more professional, there is even less ground to accuse the judges of prejudice. Nevertheless, as men they may have had great bias against women. Did these biases leak into the criminal proceedings that they directed? Before trial these men—the justices of the peace, the grand jurors, and the high court judges—heard and determined the cases of women accused of serious crime. What can we discover of their treatment of women?

The justices of peace were better off financially and far more learned than the ordinary townsmen in the county. Most of the justices, by virtue of long service, dealt with many cases of minor offenses. In these they may have given vent to feelings of bias against women, the "weaker vessel, in both body and mind."[2] From the extant record, however, there is little evidence that they extended this view to women accused of more serious offenses. Instead there is a solemnity and fairness about the formal steps from interrogation to trial.

Very often the first and decisive report of a female's crime was brought to the justice by another woman. In this way the entire community, male and female, showed that suspicions of serious crimes were not held back by anyone. Bethiah Wharton's testimony in Margaret Callegharne's infanticide case gives detailed evidence of a community-magistrate partnership in ferreting out crimes. Her deposition described the discovery of a crime and how it was brought to the court's attention. Wharton swore that

> on or about [ ] January going with Ruth Ripno who was then anursing in the house to make the bed of Margareet Callegharne who had kept her bed the greatest part of the day before by reason of a pain in her leg as she said occasioned by a fall in the street but when we came found her gone for which reason with some others gave us great cause of suspicion that she had had a child which put us upon searching narrowly for it where we found her up two pair of stairs but found none there but afterwards being in the chamber where she lay with Mrs. Mary Catta who examined her whether she had had a child . . . which she utterly deneyed but in little time after Mrs. Catta spying something under the bed asked me what cloath that was there upon which I looked under the bed and see something and pulled out the cloath which by the bigness and weight of it I supposed be child upon which I told her I

had found something and asked her whether it was born alive she told me it was not[.] I then desired Mrs. Catta to take and open the cloath which she refused saying she did not know whether it was safe to doe it upon which Mrs. Mercy Rolstone and Mrs. Mary Gibbs was sent for who was desired to open it to whom I . . . refer you for father information for I was not present when they opened it.[3]

Midwives and matrons did, in the course of their neighborly rounds, come across evidence of crime, particularly that of women who had lately given birth. A special oath required them to bring to light any irregularities in childbearing.[4]

In Mary Flood's case, neighbors sitting in the next room reported a child's cries and the appearance of a distraught Mary. She wailed to them: "I have killed my child."[5]

Depositions of witnesses and defendants, given before magistrates and coroners and included in the trial file papers, hint that the justices occasionally acted on mere rumor. When information reached the court in 1684 that Sarah Osborne had reported to someone "that she knew a woman that lately had a child born of her body, that was privately buryed, and no knowledge taken thereof, which gives suspition that some horrid wickedness hath bin perpetrated and concealed," an investigation commenced. The justices ordered "the constables of the city . . . to bring in Sarah Osborne for questioning."[6]

On other occasions a case of felony might come to the high court by way of an inferior court's investigation of a lesser crime. Such was a 1674 case with "Nan" or "Anna." The keeper of the prison in Boston, Thomas Matson, was ordered "to take into [his] custody ye person of Nan Negro slave to Mrs. Rebecca Lindes of Charlestowne, she being under ye conviction of haveing had a bastard, & being under verry sore suspicion of makeing it away, she not being able to give any satisfactory account of its death, and haveing received her you are to keep her in safe custody til ye Court of Assistance [*sic*] next ensueing."[7]

Once a suspected crime was reported, the magistrates—or the justices of the peace after 1692—decided whether to bind the suspect over for trial. Occasionally a judge, as in the 1673 accusation of witchcraft leveled by Samuel Bennett and his wife against Anna Edmunds in the Court of Assistants, dismissed the charges as unfounded.[8] The suspect was then freed by order "that she go." If securities were taken for her appearance, she and those who put up bond with her were "discharged" by proclamation. Between the time the accusation was made and the suspect's appearance in court, the accuser might fail to appear to press the accusation. This happened in the 1691 case of Elizabeth Fanning, the only woman accused of treason. At the October meeting of the Court of Assistants, "after Proclamation by an Oyes, three times made in Court," no one came forward to press the charge against her.[9] Sarah Marlington, having been committed for trial and brought before the May 1702 meeting of the Superior Court in Boston, was discharged by proclamation when no one appeared to prosecute her for theft.[10] In 1699 Katherine Price, servant to the Boston prisonkeeper, was apprehended while aiding Joseph Bradish, a suspected pirate, to escape, but she was discharged without being formally charged.[11]

Homicide was the least likely offense to go unreported or unrecognized, partly because a suspicious death required an investigation and the court commissioned juries of inquest to examine the body to determine the cause of death. Coroners, as in England, presided.[12] In Margaret Fennison's case, an inquest was held at Malden under the auspices of "Joseph Phillips Gent. One of the coroners of our said Lord the King":

> upon view of the Body of an Infant male child about a year old (as we Judge then and there being Dead, . . .) [the fourteen member jury of inquest were] charged and sworn to Enquire for our said Lord the King, when by what means and how the said Child came to his Death upon their oaths do say that the said child by some Person (unknown to us) within a week past was wilfully and Feloniously Kill'd and murder'd against the Peace of our Sovereign Lord the King . . . first by Bruising him on the Head and then fastning a stone about the Body of him about three pound weight and [illegible] in a clay pit in Malden aforesaid.[13]

An inquest could result in a finding of deliberately induced death either by a particular person or by an unknown hand, or it might conclude that the victim died of an accident or natural causes, as was the case with the inquest of the dead infant bastard of Sarah Goldthwaite.[14]

Another jury that might be called to rule on physical evidence—unique to cases involving women—was the jury of matrons or midwives. Such a jury was called to examine Elizabeth Emmerson for signs of giving birth. The four women who made their marks on the deposition swore that they found such evidence. They had also examined the bodies of Emmerson's dead twin infants and testified that the children died from smothering. These knowledgeable, though illiterate, women gave expert testimony on questions of birth and death.[15]

Magistrates before the second charter and single justices of the peace after 1692 were empowered to call witnesses, take testimony on oath, and supply it to the courts. English and colonial law and precedent gave great discretion to justices in this regard.[16] In serious crimes the testimony of witnesses was crucial to the prosecution, but as a document in the files of the Rebecca Chamblit infanticide case of 1733 shows, sometimes witnesses did not appear. Four of the seven potential witnesses were examined, but another three were "not to be foun'd." These witnesses were required to testify before a bill could be brought by the grand jury.[17] The defendant and her family as well as neighbors and passersby might also be questioned before the matter came to a trial. In 1678 Cardin Drabstone's family was interrogated about the death and burial of her bastard child; partly because of their deposition at her trial that the child was premature and born dead, Cardin was acquitted of murder.[18] In the case of Elizabeth Emmerson, both she and her parents were thoroughly questioned. Emmerson was interrogated "as she lay upon her bed" after her dead twins were unearthed. A sample of the questioning shows that the examining justice was well informed about the case and her previous life:

Q: What is yo[ur] Husbands name?
A: I have never an [*sic*] one.
Q: Were you ever married?
A: No: never.
Q: Have you not been a second time delivered, & had Two Children or Twins this month?

A: Yea, I have.
Q: Did you not do them to death by violence, sitting down upon them smothering them or by any other means?
A: No: by no means at all.
Q: Who helped you sow them up in ye bag they were found in[?]
A: No body.

The justice doubted her protestation that no one aided her in disposing of the two children. Michael Emmerson, her father, was asked whether he had any inkling of his daughter's pregnancy. He denied any knowledge of the pregnancy and rejected any complicity in the twins' death. His wife, Hannah, was interrogated next. The justice or prosecutor was very severe.

Q: Why did you sow them up in a cloth for burial[?]
A: I did not; nor did I know of it.
Q: Did you not contrive or know of [the] buriall of them; or [undecipherable][?]
A: No:I never heard anything of it til I came almost home from [undecipherable][.]

The several hours of questioning convinced authorities to indict Elizabeth Emmerson for murder of her newborn bastards and her parents as accessories to murder.[19]

Interrogations like those of the Emmersons, Sarah Smith, and Rebecca Chamblit occurred under the most trying circumstances for the accused. Torture was not used, except perhaps in a few cases of witchcraft.[20] There were no privilege against self-incrimination and no bar to the introduction of evidence, however obtained. Examinations by justices of the peace in the locality of the crime and by prosecutors at the court sessions were read or took place before the grand jurors, for by their will alone could the prosecution progress to trial.

Thus far it is clear that the magistrates held most of the high cards in their investigation. The few rights that women had by custom or common law (against torture and other induced confessions, the right to know the charges against them, and the right to a speedy determination of the case)[21] were little counterweight against an entire criminal justice system—if indeed it was bent on ignoring exculpatory evidence or making scapegoats of them. But, with the exception of a few episodes of frenzied persecution, records of preliminary investigations do not show either consistent harassment of women by the authorities or abject submission of accused women.

We may also ask the grand jurors and the judges whether they were in league, consciously or unconsciously, to raise or lower the number of women brought to trial, according to some unspoken, general presumption about female moral capacity? The question is neither as demeaning nor as antagonistic as it appears. Motive remains a vital element in determining probable cause, and grand jurors had to decide whether a particular person was capable of committing a particular crime. Again, a careful review of all extant records does not show such intent upon the grand jurors' part. Instead, they appeared to be conscientiously seeking evidence to decide whether the suspect was a likely culprit. Grand jury indictment preceded felony trials. When a case was presented to the grand jury, its thirteen to twenty-four members, drawn from the vicinity of the crime (the county), returned their collective judgment on the validity of the charges. Their vote, unlike that of the petty (petit or small) trial jury of twelve, did not have to be unanimous—twelve votes were sufficient to bind the defendant over. The grand jury was a sturdy survival of English medieval forms. The "presenting juries"— representatives of the vills and hundreds who told the kings' justices about crimes "of their own knowledge"—were the original grand jurors.[22] The Bay Colony courts upheld the custom of vicinage: Margaret Fennison, for whom we have an unusually complete record, was first committed to Boston jail on suspicion that she murdered her eleven-month-old son. The Superior Court sent her to the Middlesex jail, where she was held for trial because the suspected crime had taken place in Malden, the county of Middlesex, rather than near her home in Boston, where she was apprehended.[23]

The king's attorney presented a bill of indictment to the grand jury in the county of the alleged crime, and the jurors returned a bill of indictment either *billa vera* (formally charging the accused with the crime under the old English formula) or *ignoramus* (allowing the suspect to go free for lack of sufficient evidence). The king's attorney could intervene in favor of a defendant or press for an indictment. After the grand jury heard the evidence on an arson charge against Sarah Bartlett and decided to indict, "the King's attorney . . . entered a Nolo prosequi," dropping the charge against her. She was then freed.[24] The wording of the true bill was the same for nearly all cases, with the details of the particular case inserted in the appropriate place. The indictment of Pegg in the Superior Court in 1761 is typical.

> The Jurors for the Lord the King for this County upon their Oath did present that Pegg a negrowoman of Swansey in the County of Bristol a servant for term of life to Josephy Swasey of Swansey aforesaid mariner not having the fear of god before her eyes but being instigated by the Devil on the first day of November last past at Swansey aforesaid with force and arms feloniously, wilfully, and of her malice aforethought assaulted her female negro Child named Violet of about the age of four years in the peace of god and the Lord the King then & there being and that the said pegg then and there with force as aforesaid feloniously willfully & of her malice aforethought did take and carry from the dwelling house of the said Joseph Swasey her aforesaid female child Violet and did then and there throw the said female child into the water in the great River in Swansey aforesd, near the dwelling house of the said Joseph Swasey and thereby the same female child the said pegg then and there feloniously willfully and of the malice aforethought by throwing into the River aforsd. did Suffocate Strangle and drown of which suffocation strangling and drowning the sd. female child then and there instantly died and so the jurors aforesaid upon their Oath aforesaid Say'd that the said pegg her aforesaid female child Violet feloniously willfully and of her malice aforethought killed and murdered against the peace of the said Lord the King his crown & Dignity.[25]

The formula followed in these indictments covered the essential legal elements for attributing culpability.[26] The defendant was identified, and evil intent (*mens rea*) was attributed to her. Over and over again the indictment reiterates the premeditated malice the accused had in relation to the criminally proscribed result. Premeditated malice—specific intent—was necessary for a charge of murder. The defendant was then charged with the positive act—*actus reus*—of assaulting the victim. This act was willful behavior. The formula continued to complete the requirements for criminal culpability by making the *actus reus*—the assault itself—the cause of the child's death. The causation was spelled out: the child's death was the immediate result of the assault by the mother, and no intervening cause obviated the woman's responsibility. Finally, the indictment concluded with the exact charge the grand jurors decided to bring against the accused, in this case murder.

In addition to the legal elements of criminal culpability—*mens rea, actus reus,* and causation—the indictment had to include the identity of the suspect and the victim, the details of the offense(s), and the correct date(s) of all that took place. In England omissions or errors in the merest details of the indictment could lead to its challenge by the defendant and a directed dismissal of the charges.[27] In cases before the Superior Court of Judicature this rarely occurred, but a previous acquittal, a lack of a formal indictment, or a mistaken identity did serve to free defendants. The crucial issue was occasionally the *corpus delecti*—the legal requirement that proof of the existence of a crime be presented. In homicides this was the corpse; in robbery, proof of the victim's prior possession of the article and the suspect's later possession or disposal of it. Without the *corpus delecti* there was no crime.[28] Counsel could be appointed or retained to assist the accused upon the law in these indictments, particularly when the offenses were capital, but evidence of lawyer's intervention in these cases is hard to obtain.[29] Instead, the awesome authority of the court and the understandable fear of the defendant to give offense to the judges combined to reduce the frequency of challenges to the indictment.

Grand jurors did not always bring a true bill against a woman charged with a serious crime. When the king's attorney general exhibited a bill of indictment to the Boston grand jury in March 1732 against Hannah Roberts, the wife of mariner Thomas Roberts, the bill was returned *ignoramus*.[30] The defendant had still to be dismissed by the court from her recognizance. The Essex grand jury in 1702 found no bill against Margaret Lambert, who had been accused of "the detestable sin of incest" with her brother. However, Lambert, at hand when the "no bill" was returned, suddenly confessed "that She was never married, had had a Child born of her Body that her Brother James Lambert was the Father of the Child." The judges summarily ordered that she be whipped twenty stripes. Evidently an indictment was not necessary when a suspect confessed.[31] Incest was no longer a capital offense, but the judges' summary intervention and the sentence of corporal punishment suggest that they believed her conduct merited severe punishment.

Though Margaret Lambert stood in court while the grand jury voted upon her indictment, the defendant did not always appear at this stage. In May 1724, the Suffolk grand jury returned an indictment against Margaret Chaplin for passing counterfeit currency, "but Inasmuch as the Court is Informed that the sd. Margaret Chaplin had kept hid so that she could not be found to make answer," a warrant was issued for her apprehension.[32] Chaplin was tried the following February and acquitted. The vast majority of defendants were in custody when the grand jury heard their cases.

Finally, even when the grand jury named a person in an indictment and the prosecutor did not move to drop prosecution, the proceedings against that individual occasionally failed to materialize. In 1760 Meriam Ashley was indicted by the Hampshire grand jury for counterfeiting coin. She was specifically cited as an accessary, for providing the copper kettle used to melt down the coin. Still in custody, Ashley was not mentioned again in the trial record, while her male accomplices were convicted and sentenced. For some reason she was not prosecuted, though the grand jury had found probable cause of her culpability. Ashley had previously been brought before the court on a charge of counterfeiting and, though convicted, was sentenced to the extremely mild punishment of a £3 fine. As a recidivist, she might have been the object of severe penalties in the 1760 case, but she was not.[33]

Cases of serious crime might also have come to the highest court upon appeal of a county court decision. For example, Joseph Younglove appealed a conviction for theft in the Hampshire Superior Court because he had not been indicted by the grand jury for the county. He brought a copy of the county court record to the Superior Court of Judicature (the appellate court for the colony) and was ordered discharged. Cases brought to the Superior Court in this way were usually tried anew before the judges and a jury.[34] In 1707 Mary Smith, wife of James Smith, was indicted by the grand jury of the county of Barnstable for concealing stolen money. Jeremiah Gatchill, a wheelwright, claimed that James Smith had taken the money, and Mary refused to give it back to Gatchill. The county court found her guilty, and Mary appealed the decision. A jury at the Superior Court heard the case anew and found Mary Smith not guilty.[35]

The role of the judges who sat upon the principal court bench must not be minimized. Unlike the modern American trial court judges, who preside and rule, colonial judges followed an English model. They often intervened in trials, to address the defendant, the king's attorney, the witnesses, and the trial jurors. They not only determined points of law but also pursued matters of fact. Drawn from the elite of the colony, were they also secret harborers of misogynistic prejudice? Or did they merely share the condescending view of women expressed by the founders of the colony?

The Superior Court consciously functioned as a high court, presumably above petty prejudices, politics, and pleadings. (The only occasion upon which the judges fell prey to local considerations occurred during the Salem witch trials.) The class from which the justices were drawn was not exempt from antifeminine feelings, but the justices were hardly Savonarolas. The Sewalls, Lynds, Winthrops, Olivers, and Hutchinsons who sat upon the court were not always professional lawyers, but they were the elite of the colony. By and large, they were men of learning, sense, and respect for the law.[36] They appear to have accepted the view of crimes expressed by almost all criminal jurists in the century from Matthew Hale to Cesare Beccaria: it was not the criminal who mattered in judgment, but the crime. In moments when society was threatened by a particular class of criminals committing a particular type of crime, the social order-keeping view of the administration of criminal law might lead to persecution of a sect, class, or gender, but in the absence of a specific threat, it could be quite blind to the characteristics of the accused.

In addition, although the judges remained on the high

court bench for life—and some were very long-lived indeed—
the professional quality of judging changed over time. By the
mid-eighteenth century the Puritan court had largely given
way to a court of trained lawyers. This gradual shift, which
continued through the end of the century, directly affected
defendants. As intrusive as the judges were in the conduct of
criminal trials, their orientation and their approach to the role
of judging had great bearing upon cases. As the judges at the
Salem witchcraft trials proved, Puritan religious convictions
could override common law rules of judging when the judges
were more Puritan magistrates than legal experts. And the
seventeenth-century Court of Assistants was not dominated by
lawyers but was comprised of upright, wealthy Puritan merchants and planters. The judges of the eighteenth century
were more often lawyers, whose habits at the bar they carried
to the bench. They were interested in procedural rigor in a
way that their predecessors would not have understood. This
professionalism worked against overt expressions of bias, like
those uttered by William Stoughton, the most virulent and
unrepentent of the Salem judges, throughout the witchcraft
trials. But did subtler biases—those the historian can discover
that contemporaries might have overlooked—still exist?[37]

While the same courts tried both men and women for
serious crimes, they had not the same subjective impact for
female defendants as they had for males. The judges, jurors,
officers, and counsellors were all men. A female defendant
was surrounded by men who had, literally, life and death
power over her. Any prejudice that the judges, jurors, officers, or attorneys had against female, but not against male,
defendants could not be checked by the presence of women
on the bench or at the bar. The powerlessness of the female
defendant in the court reflected her subordinate status in the
larger society. She could not hold political office, serve on
juries, or practice law. On a more intimate level, her capacity
to dispose of property, enter into contracts, obtain an education, seek employment, and even discipline her children were
subject to limitations not placed upon men. Objectively, then,
women were inferior to men, a status they brought with them
to court and saw writ large in the bench and in the jury box.

Women were also handicapped by their relative inexperience in public situations. They were not used to speaking in public, certainly not at large gatherings. Male defendants met the judges in the streets, worked with or for the jurors, served on juries themselves, sued and were sued in court, and joined in any number of public duties, including militia practice, voting, and participation in town meetings. Women did not share these activities. Some must therefore have been awed, even tongue-tied, before the raised bench of the Superior Court justices. Standing almost mute certainly did not help their causes. Whether this told in their favor, by effectively reducing them to submission to authority, or against them, by hampering their defense, it made their experience very different from men's.[38]

This isolation and naivete of women in these conditions were heightened by the hurried conduct of trials at court. All civil and criminal cases involving more than £50 sterling or life and limb could be appealed to the Superior Court, and many cases originated there as well. Women's crimes were part of a heavy load of felonies and some misdemeanors brought before the justices and their juries. Between 1673 and 1686 the Court of Assistants in its regular sessions heard thirty-four such cases, all capital offenses. The Superior Court of Judicature heard 185 cases of serious crime by women, of which 106 were capital offenses. Four women were tried in special courts of oyer and terminer within the framework of the regular high courts. Many more were tried in 1692 by special courts in Salem upon charges of witchcraft.[39] Cases went swiftly—three or four felonies were sometimes dispatched in a day. The speed of prosecution forced jurors to place more emphasis upon their judgment of the defendant and less emphasis upon any obscure points of evidence or argument that might arise. The case load blurred the individuality of cases and complexity of proofs, leaving the women in the dock standing in stark relief. In this crush of business the justices and their jurors could hardly trace the details of women's cases, unless the crime itself was notorious. Occasionally women's cases did become infamous, but this was, as we will see, a function of the crime rather than of the sex of the defendant. The result was that the crime rather than the defendant was judged.

Added to the heavy case load was the requirement, under

the second charter, that Superior Court judges ride circuit through the counties. The act that created the court specified the "places for the holding and keeping" of the Superior Court:

> Within and for the county of Suffolk, at Boston, upon the first Tuesdays in November and May; within and for the county of Essex, at Salem, on the second Tuesday in November, and at Ipswich on the third Tuesday in May; within and for the county of Middlesex, at Cambridge, on the last Tuesday in July, and at Charlestown, on the last Tuesday in January; within and for the county of Hampshire at Springfield, on the second Thursday in August; within and for the county of York, at Kittery, on the Thursday in the week next before the time herein set and appointed for the sitting of the said superior court at Ipswich; for the countys of Plymouth, Barnstable and Dukes County, at Plymouth, on the last Tuesday in March; and within and for the county of Bristol, at Bristol, on the second Tuesday in September yearly and every year from time to time.[40]

As the eighteenth century progressed, additional sessions of the court became necessary, and sittings at Barnstable, Taunton, and Falmouth were included on the court's calendar. Figure 4 shows the extent of these quarterly perambulations. It is difficult to conceive, under these conditions of coming and going, besieged with crimes and suits of such variety, how the judge could escape making extensive use of their impressions of the defendant before them, and, if these impressions were colored by bias, there was little in the swift display of evidence and brief pleading in defense to dissuade them.

Although the evidence is far from conclusive, one can argue that women accused of serious crimes could obtain defense counsel. In England the assistance of legal counsel in felony cases was not officially allowed until the early nineteenth century (except in cases of treason, where the right to counsel was granted in 1693). Counsel could be asked in matters of law, of course, but the most important contribution of trained criminal defense counsel then as now was to examine witnesses and summarize cases for the jury. Unofficially, defendants at English criminal assize courts did have lawyers

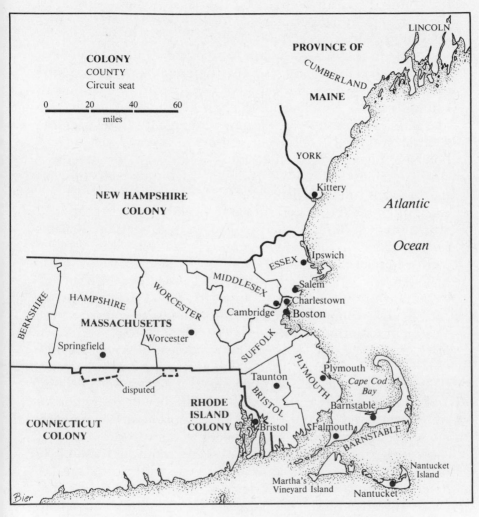

FIGURE 4. The Circuit of the Superior Court of Judicature of
Massachusetts

advise them on presentation of cases. The bench even permitted, on occasion, cross-examination and summation by criminal lawyers.[41] In Massachusetts the criminal bar played a prominent role in appealing misdemeanor convictions from the county superior courts (the courts of general sessions of the peace) to the Superior Court of Judicature. Defense counsel also appeared in felony trials heard by the high court, but their role in these cases cannot be documented with any precision. David Flaherty suggests that defendants sought counsel after they had been indicted, although the intervention of counsel can be seen even earlier in a handful of cases.[42] In Margaret Fennison's and Jemima Mangent's cases defense counsel prepared motions on matters of law and may or may not have taken part in the actual conduct of the defense.[43] The availability of defense counsel—for a fee—evidently did not prevent the conviction of women for serious crimes, though the lawyers, when they intervened, protected the legal rights of their female clients. The factual question remains unaltered by the activities of the criminal bar: were women accused of serious crimes disfavored in cases brought to the high court?

There is one last way to approach the question of prejudice against women in pretrial proceedings: to compare their treatment with that of men. For this, we need to digress into a brief theoretical discussion of the purpose and function of the criminal justice system. Our modern system provides safeguards against the innocent being arrested, indicted, tried, and convicted. The result is that the number of convictions is small compared to the number of reported offenses. Early modern criminal justice systems took a very different view of suspected crime. To authorities in these communities, the role of the criminal justice system was to suppress disorder, not to determine guilt with certitude. Figure 5 tabulates, in a flow chart, the disposition of cases for men and for women of colonial Massachusetts charged with capital offenses, from the first stage at which I have records through the trial stage. There is no significant difference between the treatment of men and women in these proceedings—almost all of them were found culpable in some way; almost all pleaded guilty. This is a near perfect example of the "crime control" model of

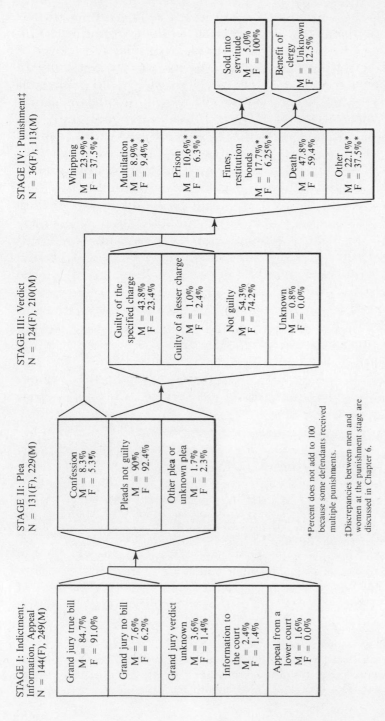

STAGE I: Indictment,
Information, Appeal
N = 144(F), 249(M)

Grand jury true bill
M = 84.7%
F = 91.0%

Grand jury no bill
M = 7.6%
F = 6.2%

Grand jury verdict
unknown
M = 3.6%
F = 1.4%

Information to
the court
M = 2.4%
F = 1.4%

Appeal from a
lower court
M = 1.6%
F = 0.0%

STAGE II: Plea
N = 131(F), 229(M)

Confession
M = 8.3%
F = 5.3%

Pleads not guilty
M = 90%
F = 92.4%

Other plea or
unknown plea
M = 1.7%
F = 2.3%

STAGE III: Verdict
N = 124(F), 210(M)

Guilty of the
specified charge
M = 43.8%
F = 23.4%

Guilty of a lesser charge
M = 1.0%
F = 2.4%

Not guilty
M = 54.3%
F = 74.2%

Unknown
M = 0.8%
F = 0.0%

STAGE IV: Punishment‡
N = 36(F), 113(M)

Whipping
M = 23.9%*
F = 37.5%*

Mutilation
M = 8.9%*
F = 9.4%*

Prison
M = 10.6%*
F = 6.3%*

Fines,
restitution
bonds
M = 17.7%*
F = 6.25%*

Death
M = 47.8%
F = 59.4%

Other
M = 22.1%*
F = 37.5%*

Sold into
servitude
M = 5.0%
F = 100%

Benefit of
clergy
M = Unknown
F = 12.5%

*Percent does not add to 100
because some defendants received
multiple punishments.

‡Discrepancies between men and
women at the punishment stage are
discussed in Chapter 6.

FIGURE 5. Disposition of Male (M) and Female (F) Capital Offenses
in Massachusetts Superior Court of Judicature, 1673–1774

a criminal justice system. Gender is not important; curbing all threats of disorder and answering all charges of crime with some sort of official hearing were the primary objectives of pretrial proceedings. Social order came before the rights of the accused. Such a view was typical of early modern criminal justice systems. As Sir William Blackstone, quoting Hale, remarked, when crime was "dangerous," "frequent," and "fearsome," the defendants' pretrial rights fell before the needs of the state.[44] Trial juries could weed out the innocent from the guilty, but no suspect should be discharged by a magistrate or a grand jury unless there was palpable evidence that he or she was not involved in the crime. Under this philosophy of criminal justice, men and women suffered alike.[45]

With or without a philosophy for controlling social disorder, the grand jurors may simply have bowed before the authority of the committing justices. At the sessions of the Superior Court of Judicature, the grand jurors were continually lectured on the obedience that they owed the justices and judges set above them. A harsh view of all serious crimes marked these addresses, and, at the same time, the sex of the defendant did not appear to make any difference.[46] Taken at face value, these charges underlined the grand jurors' willingness to indict just about everyone suspected of felony, not just, or primarily, women.

NOTES

1. For example, compare Lyle Koehler, *A Search for Power: The "Weaker Sex" in Seventeenth-Century New England* (Urbana, Ill., 1980) 227–34, on the Anne Hutchinson episode, which he sees as an example of the magistrates' sexism, with Bradley Chapin, *Criminal Justice in Colonial America* (Athens, Ga., 1983), 103–6, who regards the same affair as an exception fashioned by fear of sedition, not femininity.

2. Edmund S. Morgan, *The Puritan Family: Religion and Domestic Relations in Seventeenth-Century New England*, rev. ed. (New York, 1966), 441.

3. Callegharne's case, Suffolk court files, vol. 99, #10355 (May 5, 1715), and SCJ 1715–21, 68 (May 3, 1715).

4. The general oath for midwives required that they refrain from doing damage to a newborn, switching newborns, and harming mothers and that they report all suspicions of wrongdoing to the authorities; midwives in Massachusetts took this oath. See Thomas R. Forbes, *The Midwife and the*

Witch (New Haven, Conn., 1966), 145, and Jane B. Donegan, "Midwifery in America: 1760–1860" (Ph.D. diss., Syracuse University, 1972), 9–10.

5. A complete set of depositions to the magistrates exists for Mary Flood's case, a suspected child murder; see Suffolk court files, vol. 29, #2383–88, 82–85 (Feb., 1685).

6. Osborne's case, warrant dated Sept. 9, 1684, Suffolk court files, vol. 27, #2240, 80.

7. Anna's case, Suffolk court files, vol. 15, #1344, 56 (Mar. 2, 1674); *Court of Assistants,* 1:29–30.

8. Edmunds's case, *Court of Assistants,* 1: 11 (1673).

9. Fanning's case, ibid., 358 (Oct. 1691).

10. Marlington's case, SCJ 3:70 (May 5, 1702).

11. Price's case, SCJ 2:282 (Nov. 7, 1699).

12. On the official duties of the coroner, see R. F. Hunnisett, *The Medieval Coroner* (Cambridge, 1961), passim.

13. Fennison's coroner's inquest: Suffolk court files, vol. 31, #56937, 38–39 (May 21, 1742).

14. Goldthwaite's inquest: Suffolk court files, vol. 817, #132178; SCJ 1772, 98–99 (June 16, 1772).

15. Emmerson's jury of matrons: Suffolk court files, vol. 31, #2636, 94 (May 11, 1692).

16. On the role of the single justice, see Michael Dalton, *The Countrey Justice* (London, 1622), and John Langbein, *Prosecuting Crime in the Renaissance: England, France, Germany* (Cambridge, Mass., 1974), 21–54.

17. Chamblit's case, Suffolk court files, vol. 251, #35693, 125 (Aug. 1733).

18. Drabstone's case, Suffolk court files, vol. 15, #1211, 147 (Sept. 1678); *Court of Assistants,* 1:125.

19. Interrogation of Elizabeth Emmerson and her parents: Suffolk court files, vol. 31, #2636, 95 (May 11, 1691).

20. Torture was not unknown earlier in the English system; see John Langbein, *Torture and the Law of Proof: Europe and England in the Ancient Regime* (Chicago, 1977), 87–88. The witchcraft cases might have fit this category; certainly portions of the tactics used resembled torture; see David T. Konig, *Law and Society in Puritan Massachusetts: Essex County, 1629–1692* (Chapel Hill, N.C., 1979), 171–72. Torture was not officially used in New England courts, however.

21. Chapin, *Criminal Justice in Colonial America,* 61.

22. T. F. T. Plucknett, *A Concise History of the Commmon Law,* 5th ed. (Boston, 1956), 112, 127.

23. Fennison's warrant, Suffolk court files, vol. 31, #56937, 35–36 (June 11, 1742).

24. Bartlett's case, SCJ 1767–68, 282 (Sept. 27, 1768).

25. Pegg's case, SCJ 1760–62, 271 (Oct. 13, 1761).

26. These three elements are discussed in ch. 5, n.2.

27. J. S. Cockburn, *A History of the English Assizes, 1558–1714* (Cambridge, 1972), 117.

28. For example, see Mary Bryant's discharge upon an insufficient indictment, SCJ 1740–45, 266 (Feb. 18, 1746).

29. See William E. Nelson, *Americanization of the Common Law: The Impact of Legal Change, 1760–1830* (Cambridge, Mass., 1975), 99, and Hiller B. Zobel and L. Kinvin Wroth, eds., *The Legal Papers of John Adams* (Cambridge, Mass., 1965), 1:li–lii.

30. Roberts's case, SCJ 1730–33, 268 (Feb. 13, 1733).

31. Lambert's case, SCJ 3:76 (May 19, 1702).

32. Chaplin's case, SCJ 1721–25, 195, 263; the warrant was issued May 5, 1724, and trial was held Feb. 9, 1725.

33. Ashley's case, SCJ 1757–59, 729 (Sept. 25, 1759); SCJ 1760–62, 142–43, 262 (Sept. 23–25, 1760).

34. Nelson, *Americanization of the Common Law*, 16; Younglove's case, Suffolk court files, vol. 190, #22018, 67.

35. Smith's case, SCJ 1700–1714, 49 (May 20, 1701).

36. "Of utmost importance is it . . . that the crime and the punishment be intimately linked together." Cesare Beccaria, *On Crimes and Punishments* [1764], ed. Henry Paolucci (Indianapolis, 1963), 57. *Female Felons* is not the place to begin an extended investigation of American colonial criminological theory. Colonial justices certainly had opinions about crime, founded upon their broader views of human nature. These were not charitable to criminals. See, for example, Thomas Hutchinson's charges to the Suffolk grand juries, in Samuel Quincy's edition of Josiah Quincy Jr.'s *Reports of Cases Argued and Adjudged in the Superior Court of Judicature . . . between 1761 and 1772* (Boston, 1865), passim. With the exception of the charges to the grand juries, diary and journal entries (of which Samuel Sewall's are a fine example), and occasional reports to superiors in England, American colonial justices left these thoughts on crime inchoate. The English literature on the same subject was far more voluminous, particularly in the eighteenth century. See Leon Radzinowicz, *A History of the English Criminal Law, I: The Movement for Reform* (London, 1948), 231–67. American judges' opinions seemed to parallel those of the great English judges of the early eighteenth century: crimes were to be viewed as severe in proportion to their danger to the public order; for example, see William Blackstone, *Commentaries on the Laws of England*, 4 vols. (Oxford, 1759–65), 4:15–16. In both American and English literature little attention is paid to the individual defendant, except insofar as the law defined or limited a particular type of defendant's culpability (for example in *feme covert*). It was the crime, not the defendant, that mattered.

37. John M. Murrin, "The Legal Transformation: The Bench and Bar of 18th Century Massachusetts," in *Colonial America*, ed. Stanley N. Katz (Boston, 1971), 424–25; Chadwick Hansen, *Witchcraft at Salem* (New York, 1969), 128–29, 152–53.

38. A speculative analogy: the effect of the courtroom on slaves brought to judgment for felony in colonial Virginia was awe-inspiring by design. See Rhys Isaac, *The Transformation of Virginia, 1740–1790* (Chapel Hill, N.C., 1983), 347–49.

39. Special courts of oyer and terminer were common in other colonies, but not as common as in Massachusetts. The witchcraft cases of Salem were also *longer* in duration and dealt with a greater number of suspects. There was also the fear that the witnesses, "struck dumb," could not testify; see Thomas Newton to Isaac Addington, May 31, 1692, in Paul Boyer and Stephen Nissenbaum, eds., *The Salem Witchcraft Papers*, 3 vols. (New York, 1977), 3:867.

40. *Acts and Resolves*, 1:370–71 (1699).

41. John H. Langbein, "The Criminal Trial before the Lawyers," *University of Chicago Law Review* 45 (Winter 1978), 263–316.

42. David H. Flaherty, "Criminal Practice in Colonial Massachusetts," in *Law in Colonial Massachusetts,* Publications of the Colonial Society of Massachusetts, no. 62 (Boston, 1984), 218–19.

43. SCJ 1740–42, 264; Quincy, Jr., *Reports of Cases,* 162–63.

44. Blackstone, *Commentaries,* 4:12.

45. This "crime control" model was described by Herbert Packer and others; see Packer, *The Limits of the Criminal Sanction* (Stanford, 1968), passim.

46. See ch. 6, n. 36.

CHAPTER FIVE

WOMEN'S TRIALS AND VERDICTS IN FELONY CASES

A fair trial is the American ideal of justice. Today this means a trial conducted under the procedural safeguards of the Fourth, Fifth, and Sixth amendments of the U.S. Constitution. The rights guaranteed in these amendments were incorporated into state trial rules under the Fourteenth Amendment. In addition, individual states have granted other rights. In seventeenth- and eighteenth-century Massachusetts, fair trial meant substantial justice, meted out by fair-minded men. While defendants accused of felony had some privileges—notably the rights to a trial by jury upon an indictment by a grand jury, to defend themselves, to confront their accusers, to know in advance the charges against them and the punishments for conviction, and to have the guarantees of due process generally—in practice the burden of proof often fell upon the defendant rather than the state.[1]

Then as now the verdict of a criminal trial jury was to be based upon the legal elements of culpability—*actus reus*, a criminal act; *mens rea*, a criminal intent; and the effective causation of the crime.[2] If evidence and testimony presented to the bench or to a trial jury convinced them that a defendant knowingly and voluntarily violated the criminal law, they should find that defendant guilty. Nevertheless, as Charles Black has pointed out, "We are one and all susceptible to the tendency to see things in a better or worse light depending on our general sympathies; we fight against this, but in the end only the self-deluding think they can wholly avoid it."[3] The influence of a defendant's personal characteristics cannot be entirely ignored by judges or trial juries. Even modern legal officials are aware of these biases: "the disadvantaged are

94

more often . . . convicted" than defendants with higher status in the community.[4]

Did these biases extend back into the early history of American criminal justice, or were colonial courts harsh but essentially fair? Did judges and juries reach verdicts on the basis of factual evidence, without measurable bias against distinct groups of defendants? An alternative hypothesis can be offered in answer to these questions: that as a result of prejudicial perceptions of jurors, women (particularly single women), blacks, Indians, and servants were convicted far more frequently than other types of defendants accused of the same crimes.[5]

Trials: From Plea to Verdict

To the extent allowed by the survival of affidavits and depositions in the file papers, we can probe the trial process case by case. What women were permitted to do and how they viewed the process give clues to its fairness.

In the highest courts of Massachusetts, women pleaded not guilty in 173 of 224 cases of serious crimes; 131 were found not guilty. Eighteen confessed. Charity William, Katherine Hartnon, and Mercy Windsor all pleaded guilty to charges of felonious stealing.[6] The other option, which did not necessarily imply confession, was to choose not to contend the charges and enter a plea of *nolo contendere*. Sarah Center in 1759 and Hannah Hall in 1765 were charged with assault; both women chose not to contest the charge against them, admitting to the facts of the charge without admitting culpability. Presumably they decided it would be fruitless to contest the charges and that more serious sanctions would come when they were convicted than if they saved the court the trouble of a jury trial. Over the years defendants who confessed were less severely sentenced to corporal punishments than those who pleaded not guilty but were subsequently convicted (see Chapter 6). Or perhaps they felt that they had not done anything wrong and would not confess to a crime.[7]

The distribution of women's pleas varied according to the type of crime with which they were charged. Predictably, few women pleaded guilty to the charge of murder. The primary inducement to enter a guilty plea, the promise of a reduced sentence, was not applicable in murder cases. Surprisingly, though, three women did confess in court; their motive was almot certainly remorse. The largest percentage of women pleaded guilty to thefts, larcenies, and robberies—cases in which a reduced sentence would be likely. A few women chose to seek mercy from the justices by either admitting guilt or not contesting the charge in cases of counterfeiting, homicide, and witchcraft.

When the defendant confessed at the indictment stage or pleaded guilty at her arraignment, the justices could move very quickly against her, but only because she allowed them to do so. The indictment would be presented, she would be arraigned, plead guilty, and the justices would pronounce sentence at the same day's session. Such was the case of Elizabeth Colson, a Scituate spinster accused of killing her bastard child on May 8, 1727. In less than month she was brought to court, indicted and "upon her arraignment Pleaded Guilty, and being asked what she had to say why sentence of Death should not be passed against her Pursuant to law Declared she had nothing to say, Whereupon the Honourable Benjamin Lynde Esqr. (in the absence of the Honourable Samuel Sewall Esqr. Chief Justice) in the name of the Court, Pronounced Sentence against the Prisoner." Her execution was set for May 25.[8] The entire process took less than three weeks.

In only a few cases involving a plea of not guilty after arraignment was the defendant's trial so swift. An exception was Bettee. On March 25, 1712, Bettee, the Negro woman-servant of Isaac Winslow of Marshfield, was indicted, arraigned, tried, and sentenced to death for infanticide in a single day.[9] Few cases were heard as quickly as Bettee's. There was often delay from the return of an indictment to the arraignment and trying of a case, particularly when the highest court met in Boston, where the docket was always crowded. Mary Webster was indicted by a grand jury at the Court of Assistants in May 1683 on a charge of witchcraft but was not tried until the following September.[10] Elizabeth Emmerson's case, discussed earlier, lasted more than two years and spanned the jurisdiction of the two highest courts. Margaret Fennison also saw a number of delays in her trial, even after she was removed from Boston to Middlesex.

The large majority of women tried by the high courts of Massachusetts chose to put themselves "upon god and the country," in other words upon a jury. From 1634, they were guaranteed a jury trial in cases of felony.[11] Only five women asked to be tried before the justices without a petty jury. Abigail Johnson was one. Presented by the grand jury in 1677 for adultery, she and her accomplice, Darby Bryan, pleaded not guilty but chose to be tried by the magistrates in the Court of Assistants. If they thought the magistrates would be more inclined to believe them innocent, they were wrong. Both were found guilty and severely punished.[12]

For those who decided to place their fate in a jury of their male neighbors, there was an opportunity to challenge up to twelve of the empanelled jurors before they were sworn. Most women accepted the jurors without question, and that fact was noted in the trial record: "A Jury being called and accordingly Swoarne Noe Objection beeing made by the Prisoner." On rare occasions, such as Susannah Andrews's trial, the prisoner objected to one of the jurors "and the Challenge allowed to the prisoner."[13] Sarah Threeneedles also took exception to two of the members of her prospective jury; "the prisoner Challenge of Richard Cheever and Thomas Herring; Nathaniell Pitcher and John Hersey were put in their stead."[14]

Once the jury was sworn, the king's attorney or the victim presented the case against the accused. Sometimes the evidence included sworn depositions of witnesses taken before the trial; these witnesses might then be called to testify in person and be cross-examined by the accused or her counsel. In Sarah Threeneedles's trial it was particularly noted that "the witnesses deliver[ed] their testimony to the court (viva voce) upon their oaths." Prisoners did speak in their own defense, although not under oath, and sometimes it did them more harm than good. Threeneedles admitted in open court to being the mother of two slain infants, soon after which "the case was committed to the Jury, who went to consider of and returning into Court [did] upon their oaths say that the sd Sarah Threeneedles is guilty of the murder where of she stands indicted."[15]

The jurors took their jobs seriously and tried to be fair

when doubts arose. On occasion juries were reluctant to find the defendant guilty of the charge specified in the indictment but were equally reluctant to discharge the accused with a verdict of not guilty. Whether there was genuine disagreement by all or part of the petty jury with the precise charge set forth in the grand jury indictment, or whether they simply disagreed with the penalty prescribed for the charge under law, these jurors sometimes brought in a verdict of guilty on a reduced charge. In seven cases trial juries brought in a guilty verdict on a charge less severe than the one set forth in the indictment. For example, in theft cases the charge (and subsequent punishment) could be reduced by lowering the value of the property that was allegedly stolen.[16] In other cases juries found defendants not guilty of adultery as charged but guilty of lewd behavior, or not guilty of burglary as charged but guilty of theft.[17] In this way the jury was able to influence enormously the function of the judicial process. Trial juries could rewrite the intentions of grand juries and dictate sentences to the judges. This power of the jury in criminal cases verged upon the power to decide law as well as fact. Judges did not give extensive instruction to juries on the law, nor did they have the power to overturn jury verdicts that violated their interpretation of law.[18] Petty juries thus had some discretion to decide the charge and limit the punishment imposed on the guilty.

Even after the verdict was returned by the trial jury, women were not powerless. The defendant or her counsel could file any of several motions. In Elizabeth Eams's murder trial John Adams moved for the dismissal of charges against two of his clients named as Eams's accomplices in the murder of Ruth Eams after Elizabeth was acquitted. He knew that accessories could not be culpable if the principal was acquitted.[19] Even if the jury returned a verdict of not guilty, the defendant might have to make a motion to be discharged, as happened in the case of Anna Clarke.[20] Sometimes counsel made the motion to have an innocent client discharged. Such motions seem unnecessary once a not guilty verdict was pronounced, but the defendant remained vulnerable, as judges retained the power to impose some form of sanction against defendants even at this stage. Bethyah Gatchel, found not guilty of adultery in 1678 by a jury in the Court of Assistants, was ordered to appear to answer for lying.[21] At a "Superior Court of Assize and General Gaol Delivery" in the year 1687, Elizabeth Hollis and two male relations were acquitted of feloniously and maliciously killing sheep, "but being persons of ill fame . . . it is ordered by the Court that they stand committed untill they shall find sureties to be of the good behaviour."[22]

What can we conclude from this barebones record of what the jurors did? We can assert that women used all of the powers that any defendant had to bend the verdict to their advantage. A few confessed, hoping to seek a concession from the court. The vast majority insisted on their innocence, trusting the fairness of the jury or the strength of their alibis. The weaker sex did not swoon, which should surprise no one, but which also suggests that they had more faith in the justice of the system than do some modern scholars. But how did the jurors regard these defendants?

The social historian's capacity to determine the existence of harmful discretion—biases not warranted by evidence—in the courts of two hundred years ago is called into question in Mark Tushnet's recent essay.[23] "Tushnet's dilemma," as I call it, states that without the full transcript of a trial, showing all the evidence presented to the jury, it is extremely difficult to determine if prejudice entered jury deliberations. Statistics on conviction rates for different groups, for example, slaves and free whites, might be approximately the same but reflect very different realities. The same rate of guilty verdicts might mean that juries were trying to be fair, or that one group, against whom the jury had some animus, was indicted upon far more flimsy evidence than the second group. Equal conviction rates then mask real prejudice. Without transcripts or their equivalents, determination of jury bias is impossible. There is much to be said for Tushnet's caution on interpreting the outcomes of criminal trials. If there is a divergence in verdicts for distinct groups, one cannot always infer willful discrimination. Even though the seventeenth- and eighteenth-century criminal justice systems were the monopoly of propertied white males, one cannot deduce that numerical differences in outcomes of trials resulted from bias against the poor and the disenfranchised. Small numerical variations may even be a by-product, in some way we cannot fathom, of incomplete records. Few colonies boast complete runs of criminal courts records; in fewer cases still are the extant records accompanied by file papers. How then can we begin to find out whether the discrimination we discern in modern courts has roots in our distant past?

While defendant faced them, jurors listened to evidence, weighed testimony, plumbed the character of witnesses and accused, and finally gave a verdict. How did the jurors reach their decision? Again, as Tushnet has warned, without the trial transcript, the scholar cannot know all that the jury knew. To extend Tushnet's argument beyond the place where he let it rest, let's ask the question: without the defendant and the witnesses before them, how can scholars see what the jury saw?

Verdicts

The answer lies in more complete quantification of surviving court records. From extant dockets and records we can compile data on the number and characteristics of crimes and the personal features of defendants. If we find overwhelming discrepancies in verdicts given to different types of defendants, whether separated by race, gender, marital status, or condition of servitude, we may begin to claim that prejudice is affecting the outcome of trials. If, for example, 100 percent of all female defendants were found guilty of felonies and 100 percent of male defendants were acquitted, even Tushnet would agree that misogyny influenced verdicts. Such an extreme correlation does not exist in the real world, but to the extent that the records show strong correlations of this sort, we can assign some causal role to prejudice. Conversely, if correlations are weak, we cannot sustain a case for prejudice without far more complex speculations about the meaning of our figures. As Michael Hindus has proposed, "Only a substantial variation in jury treatment of criminal cases . . . without retrying cases from the hindsight of at least a century . . . constitutes convincing evidence that differences were not the result of either ruthless or incompetent prosecutors."[24]

Table 7 shows a weak relationship between the gender of

TABLE 7. Verdict by Sex in Capital Offenses

		Sex		
		Female	Male	Row Total
Verdict	Not guilty	93	114	207
	Guilty	39	94	133
	Column Total	132	208	340

Note. Q = .326. Chi-squared for this table is sufficiently high (8.301) to assure us (at the 99 percent level of significance) that this weak relationship is not a random result.

the accused and the verdict of the trial jury. Overall we can state that for all of the capital cases between 1673 and 1774, there was little but nevertheless discernible discrimination in verdicts on the basis of sex.

When these aggregate numbers are broken down to show change over time, an interesting pattern emerges, with an important shift after 1700 (Figure 6). The seventeenth century saw a higher percentage of female-than male convictions and strikingly dissimilar patterns of conviction. This is particularly true for the 1690s, when the male percentage declined and the female percentage dramatically increased, almost inversely. The eighteenth century saw male conviction percent-

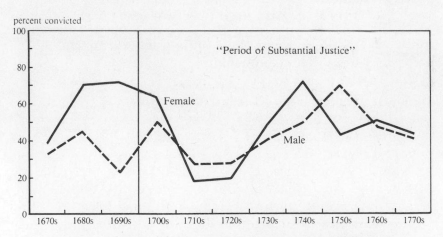

FIGURE 6. Male and Female Effective Conviction Rates in Massachusetts, 1673–1774 (includes "no bills," guilty pleas, and reductions of charges)

ages rise above female percentages, and, equally important, both moved in a parallel path for the next seventy years. Thus discrimination against women may have existed in the earlier period, but after the aberrant decade of the 1690s even-handed justice seems to have been the rule.

Beyond gender, the single most obvious personal characteristic of the accused is race. Table 8 shows a moderate relationship between guilty verdicts and race. Again, this result is statistically significant. We can therefore be reasonably sure

TABLE 8. Verdict by Race in Capital Offenses

		Race		Row Total
		White	Black	
Verdict	Not guilty	149 (65.1%)	12 (42.9%)	161
	Guilty	80 (34.9%)	16 (57.1%)	96
	Column total	229 (100%)	28 (100%)	257

Note. Q = .426. Chi-squared = 5.259; significance at the 97.5 percent level.

that there is a moderate relationship between being black and being found guilty. When the combined figures for males and females are disaggregated, this pattern subtly changes. Table 9 shows a strong relationship between race of the female and verdict. Predictably, the relationship between race of the male and verdict is quite weak, thus diluting the correlation when males and females are combined.

TABLE 9. Verdict by Race in Capital Offenses, Females Only

		Race		Row Total
		White	Black	
Verdict	Not guilty	78	5	83
	Guilty	21	7	28
	Column total	99	12	111

Note. Q = .677. Chi-squared = 7.819; significance at the 99 percent level. A comparison of verdicts for Indians and whites showed no relationship at all: Q = .112, chi-squared = .445.

In almost every indictment the occupational status of the defendant was noted.[25] For women, in most cases, occupation was largely a question of marital status (see the discussion below). One exception was women who were indentured servants or slaves, which was carefully recorded. If there was a sharp class distinction based upon occupation, one that might have prejudiced free landholding trial jurors, it was that of servitude. I have divided men and women defendants into the simple categories of servant and non-servant. Servants include all those designated as servants or slaves in the record (slaves were only a small number of the total). The non-servant category includes all professions (free laborer, yeoman, merchant, mariner, among others, for men) and all women identified by marital status with no mention of servitude or profession. Table 10 shows a moderate relationship between servitude and verdict. Though servants were almost equally likely to be found guilty or not guilty, non-servants were convicted in only one-third of their cases. This is not a strong correlation—and it would be rash to overstate the relationship between servitude and verdict—but neither is this a random result.

TABLE 10. Verdict by Male and Female Occupation

		Occupation		
		Servant	Non-Servant	Row Total
Verdict	Not guilty	20	141	161
	Guilty	22	66	88
	Column total	42	207	249

Note. $Q = -.403$. Chi-squared $= 6.419$; significance at the 95 percent level. The number of servants is considerably smaller than the number of non-servants here. It should not be concluded that this supports the idea that servants escaped discrimination in criminal prosecutions because so many more non-servants were indicted and tried. Servants were only 16.9 percent of the defendants, and they were also only a small proportion of the population at large.

When servitude is disaggregated by sex, an interesting distinction emerges: male servants were more likely to be convicted of capital offenses than female servants (63.6 percent of men, 40 percent of women). This difference in verdict is not caused by the intervening variable of sex, for the disaggregation fits the picture of male and female convictions generally. Servants are merely typical of the general population.

These differentials may be affected by the intervening variable of race, as most blacks and Indians indicted were servants. In other words, when we conclude that servants were more likely to be convicted, we may simply be testing the effect of race under another label. Table 11 shows the distribution of verdicts of white and black servants. Whatever small difference there might be in verdicts between white and black servants, it is not great enough to explain the much larger difference between servants and non-servants generally.

TABLE 11. Verdict by White and Black Servants, Males and Females

		Servants		Row Total
		White	Black	
Verdict	Not guilty	6	10	16
	Guilty	6	16	22
	Column total	12	26	38

Note. Q = .230.

Women were identified in indictments most often by their marital status, not occupation. Table 12 tests the hypothesis that single women were viewed as inherently less moral and thus more likely to be guilty of crimes. The category of single women includes single, widowed, separated, and divorced

TABLE 12. Verdict by Female Marital Status, Capital and Non-Capital Offenses

		Marital Status		Row Total
		Single	Married	
Verdict	Not guilty	60	42	102
	Guilty	36	22	58
	Column total	96	64	160

Note. Q = −.068.

women. Not included in the table are twenty-two women whose marital status is unknown and forty-two women for whom there were "no bills," special verdicts, or pleas of guilty. Overall, there was no relationship between a woman's marital status and the trial verdict. Single women were at no disadvantage before trial juries in colonial Massachusetts, except, as we have seen, in the seventeenth century and then only when they were charged with certain types of crimes.[26]

The final distinct characteristic that may have influenced jurors, regardless of evidence, is the type of charge in the indictment. Were trial juries more or less likely to find a defendant guilty when the charge was a capital crime? To some extent this category indicates the degree to which procedural safeguards were applied and juries were empathetic to the plight of the accused. Table 13 compares female capital and non-capital cases by verdict. There is no doubt that the nature of the charge did affect verdict. Juries were less likely to convict a woman of a capital offense. And this result is not random. Juries in colonial Massachusetts simply did not feel that the social control of deviance was worth an easy application of the death penalty.

TABLE 13. Verdict by Female Capital and Non-Capital Cases

| | | Type of Offense | | |
		Capital	Non-Capital	Row Total
Verdict	Not guilty	93	18	111
	Guilty	39	23	62
	Column total	132	41	173

Note. Q = .506. Chi-squared = 9.591; significance at the 99 percent level.

Juries did not see a case as simply male-female, white-black, or capital–non-capital. The defendant and case were judged as a whole, and so characteristics overlapped in the minds of jurors. How much each individual characteristic contributed to the jurors' decision, as well as how these characteristics may have combined to influence verdicts, can be determined by the statistical procedure known as Multiple Classification Analysis (MCA).

All of the technical apparatus of the MCA has been placed in Appendix 2, but the results can be simply summarized here. When the marital status and race of the accused are taken into account simultaneously with the severity and type of the offense, with MCA we can measure the effect of any one variable upon the verdict and hold the others constant. Of course, this is a statistical fiction, a probability of a guilty verdict, rather than actual verdicts. Nevertheless, the results we obtained by using this sophisticated computer technique confirm our earlier conclusions. Isolated from race and crime, marital status had very little relationship to verdict. Indeed, only one variable had any real relationship to verdict: the nature of the offense, capital or non-capital. If death was the penalty, the jurors tended to find a defendant guilty far less often than when the penalty was not death. Together, these variables did have some measurable impact upon the verdict, as one would expect from the strongest single indicators of jury decision-making. A second MCA, comparing men and women, demonstrates, as we would expect, that men's verdicts did not significantly differ from women's for the same crime. The gross difference was a function of the different sorts of crimes for which the two sexes were tried.

Firm conclusions about the effects of the characteristics of defendants and crimes upon conviction for serious crimes are difficult because one can never actually penetrate the minds of jurors. Some defendants undoubtedly escaped conviction because the jurors decided that such a person could not have committed such a crime. Nevertheless, in part, these highly personal judgments can be reconstructed for the mass of defendants, if not in every case, by statistical comparisons among a large number of variables that reflect the characteristics of defendants, types of crimes, and verdicts.

What emerges is a picture of substantial justice crisscrossed with lines of prejudice. Certain crimes and the race and servitude of the accused did play a role in labeling likely suspects and encouraging convictions. But given the prevalence of racial and gender bias in other areas of eighteenth-century life, the result is surprisingly mild. More interesting is that conviction patterns showed so little concern for personal characteristics. On the whole, women (regardless of marital status), male blacks (charged with capital offenses), and Indians were not substantially disfavored by the courts' verdicts. That modern pattern of prejudice identified by social scientists in our contemporary criminal justice system cannot be said to be inherently part of the system historically. Eighteenth-century Massachusetts juries applied substantial justice to men and women.

NOTES

1. This was fully in conformity with English practice, wherein the crown had great latitude and the defendant stood almost alone. See J. H. Baker, "Criminal Courts and Procedure at Common Law, 1550–1800," in *Crime in England, 1550–1800*, ed. J. S. Cockburn (London, 1977), 15–48, and Cockburn, *A History of the English Assizes 1558–1774* (Cambridge, 1972), 120–21. Nevertheless, a Massachusetts bill of rights, of sorts, was passed in 1691; it was disallowed by the Privy Council. See *Acts and Resolves*, 1:41.

2. Robert W. Ferguson and Allan H. Stokke, *Concepts of Criminal Law* (Boston, 1979), 113–44.

3. Charles L. Black, Jr., *Capital Punishment: The Inevitability of Caprice and Mistake* (New York, 1974), 91.

4. For example, Steven B. Boris, "Stereotypes and Dispositions for Criminal Homicide," *Criminology* 17 (Aug. 1979), 148; Marvin E. Wolfgang and Bernard Cohen, *Crime and Race* (New York, 1970), especially 80–81; Freda Adler and Rita James Simon, eds., *The Criminology of Deviant Women* (Boston, 1979), editors' introduction, 249, 250.

5. William M. Wiecek, "The Statutory Law of Slavery and Race in the Thirteen Mainland Colonies of British America," *William and Mary Quarterly*, 3d ser., 34 (Apr. 1977), 276. Julius Goebel, Jr., and T. Raymond Naughton, *Law Enforcement in Colonial New York: A Study in Criminal Procedure* (New York, 1944), 382, argue that trial was essentially fair. One must note that race, rather than gender, is the subject of these authors' remarks upon procedural fairness.

6. William's case, SCJ 1:12 (Nov. 2, 1686); Hartnon's case, SCJ 1:18 (Apr. 26, 1687); Windsor's case, SCJ 1:19 (Apr. 26, 1687).

7. Center's case, SCJ 1757–59, 654–55 (Aug. 7, 1759); Hall's case, SCJ 1764–65, 274 (Sept. 17, 1765).

8. Colson's case, SCJ 1725–29, 111 (Apr. 25, 1727).

9. Bettee's case, SCJ 1700–1714, 270 (Mar. 25, 1712).

10. Webster's case, *Court of Assistants*, 1:229–33 (indicted May 22, 1683, tried Sept. 1683).

11. Nathaniel Shurtleff, ed., *Records of the Governor and Company of the Massachusetts Bay*, 4 vols. (Boston, 1852–64), 1:118 (1634).

12. Johnson's case, *Court of Assistants*, 1:115 (1677).

13. Andrew's case, SCJ 1686–1700, 47, 50 (Mar. 10, 1696). Actually, two trial juries of twelve men each were sworn for criminal cases; they took turns hearing cases. When a juror on one of the juries was challenged, his place was simply taken by a juror from the other panel.

14. Threeneedles's case, SCJ 2:199–200 (Oct. 1698).

15. Ibid.

16. See Grafton's case, SCJ 1747–50, 275 (Aug. 15, 1749). English juries regularly reduced thefts to less than 10d. to prevent capital punishment. Massachusetts law did not make burglary and highway robbery capital offenses until the 1710s. On the reduction of charges from grand to petty theft in England, see Cockburn, *History of the English Assizes*, 97. This was regularly done in the colonies as well; see Goebel and Naughton, *Law Enforcement in Colonial New York*, 674–75, 751.

17. A case in point: De Caster's case, SCJ 1736–38, 209 (Aug. 8, 1738).

18. William E. Nelson, *Americanization of the Common Law: The Impact of Legal Change, 1760–1830* (Cambridge, Mass., 1975), 3–4, but see also Hiller B. Zobel and L. Kinvin Wroth, eds., *The Legal Papers of John Adams* (Cambridge, Mass., 1965), 1:xlix.

19. Eams's case, SCJ 1769, 221 (Nov. 7–15, 1769); Adams's motion is at 222.

20. Clarke's case, SCJ 1772, 187 (Oct. 27, 1772).

21. Gatchel's case, *Court of Assistants*, 1:138 (1678).

22. Hollis's case, SCJ 1:20 (Apr. 26, 1687).

23. Mark Tushnet, "Major Themes in the History of the Criminal Law in the United States," a paper presented at the Conference on the History of Crime, University of Maryland, College Park, Sept. 4, 1980.

24. Michael Stephen Hindus, *Prison and Plantation: Crime, Justice, and Authority in Massachusetts and South Carolina, 1767–1878* (Chapel Hill, N.C., 1980), 90.

25. Occupation was a standard entry on indictments. It was used in the era before Social Security numbers to help insure that the person being tried was the person sought for the crime.

26. While this was true overall, unmarried women were at a disadvantage when they were accused of certain crimes, particularly those involving immodesty and immoral sexual conduct. These, with witchcraft, were viewed more sternly by juries during the seventeenth century. The reverse seems to be true of such cases after the 1700s.

CHAPTER SIX

SENTENCE AND PUNISHMENT
OF WOMEN FOR FELONY

Throughout the first part of this book, we have seen how the law not only expressed the consensus of the people but also labeled the behavior of a few of those people as dangerously deviant. In this chapter we reverse the direction of the argument and proceed from the individual to the community. The last stage of the criminal justice system dealt with those convicted of crime: their sentences and punishments. It was a stage of the justice process that had two functions. The first made the guilty suffer for their crimes. The variety of sentences prescribed, even in capital cases, indicated that the judges had discretion in sentences that followed rough classifications of the severity of the offense. The characteristics of the defendants had little effect upon sentences. The court acted as agent of the state and, more indirectly, of the deity in punishing the guilty, a task that supplanted the aim of discretionary justice. The second purpose of punishment was to give a lesson to the community. Punishment was public, so that the community could see and join in the shame and pain of the accused. These two functions—retribution and public admonishment to deter—were woven into the very fabric of Massachusetts criminal justice. An examination of how they operated with regard to women completes this study of female felons.

Punishment was the last step in the criminal justice process. If only a small minority of those suspected, indicted, and prosecuted ever reached this stage, it was for these women the most rueful part of the process. Only eighty-six women were convicted by the Court of Assistants and Superior Court of Judicature for serious crimes and so became liable to punishment. Of these, only thirty-eight women were convicted for capital offenses. These instances of punishment, though few in number, were extremely important in terms of the process of applied justice in early Massachusetts.

Women faced a variety of punishments in the colonial high courts. Often these punishments would appear together; more than one kind of punishment might be prescribed by the justices for a single case. For the sake of analysis the frequencies of various punishments are discussed as distinct entities, yet it should be remembered that many times two or more of these types of sanctions were combined against the individual. The general severity of a woman's sentence was fairly consistent among the various punishments applied: if she were sentenced to pay a large fine, the number of stripes and the bond she would have to produce would be similarly high. The converse was also true; small fines were combined with fewer lashes.

The least severe sanction was the requirement that a woman post a bond and provide sureties for good behavior for a specified time. Only eight women were required to provide bond: five had to post £25 or less, and three were required to provide bonds of over £50. One of these was Meriam Fitch, convicted of larceny against Boston shopkeeper Christopher Clark in 1763. She and her accomplice were identified by the court as "persons of very ill fame and dishonest conversation and common deceivers and defrauders," and the court felt justified in requiring her to post £100 with two sureties of £50 each to insure her good behavior for twelve months.[1] Twelve months was an extended length of time for the court to hold a bond. Four-fifths of those who posted a bond for a stated length of time were merely asked to provide bond until the next term of the court, usually three to four months. A year was not the longest period of time required by the court for a bond, however. Mary Richards was required to post £100 with two sureties of £50 each for a period of three years for a conviction for fraud. In 1750 she and a male accomplice in a bold scheme extorted £300 by sending a letter to their victim threatening arson if the sum was not paid.[2]

Two kinds of financial penalties were prescribed by the courts for thefts and other crimes against property. The first was restitution and damages to the victim, and the second was a fine paid to the crown. Sarah Young, a widow of Charlestown, convicted in 1762 of stealing £20 worth of linen and clothes, was required to pay Sarah Newhall treble damages of £60, the returned goods counting for one-third of the amount.[3] The next year in Boston Margaret Waters was sentenced to pay treble damages to Samuel Allen for the theft of £12 worth of clothes from his house.[4] Thirteen women were sentenced to pay fines from under £10 to over £50. Most of these women paid fines between £20 and £50, and one woman was required to pay a fine of over £50. This last was Sabina, "servant or slave" to Richard Saltonstall of Haverhill, who in 1709 robbed and then blew up the house of her master. Despite the pleas of her confederate, Tom, who offered to pay the money back to save her from punishment, she was required to "pay the treasury of the colony" the sum of £168 as well as £12 to her master.[5] Mary Richards, in addition to the long term for her large bond, was required to pay a fine of £50. Her husband, Samuel Richards, petitioned that the fine on his wife be moderated, and the court ruled that £20 of the fine be remitted.

There were six occasions when women could not pay their fines or provide the necessary bond, and these women faced the possibility of being sold into service. Jemimah Terry could not pay treble damages to widow Ann Griffiths of Boston after her conviction in 1743 for the felonious stealing of £50 worth of clothes and bills of credit. The court ordered that Griffiths could sell Terry's service for a period of seven years.[6] Sarah Trefy was likewise disposed in service to cover £82/3/6 in damages she owed Jeremiah Lee, "Esq.," after she was found guilty of stealing some Irish linen and hats from his Marblehead warehouse in 1767.[7] Richard Foster's former maid, Jude Shepard, was required to return as his servant to cover £22/10 in damages she owed him for stealing some silk and lace when she left his service in 1696.[8] Boston spinster Mary Bushell barely avoided a six-year term of service in 1748 after making an arrangement with her victim, Boston merchant Ralph Inman.[9] Sabina, despite Tom's offer, could not meet the economic sanctions imposed upon her; the court, adding this to the severity of her arson, ordered that she be sold beyond the sea. This was also applied as a punishment in itself against particularly dangerous slave women. Coffee, the black slave of William Shaw of Little Compton, was "sold and transported into some [of] Her Majesty's Plantations" for a near-fatal assault with a knife on her mistress in 1713. The court cautioned her that should she ever return to the colony, she would face imprisonment for life.[10] In these cases the Massachusetts high courts followed the example of the English jail delivery courts by transporting convicts who would otherwise be executed. Massachusetts received very few English convicts, but the southern colonies were flooded with them in these same years.[11]

Imprisonment was not a common punishment in eighteenth-century Massachusetts, particularly for women.[12] It was reserved for only a handful of incorrigibles who were thought by the court to be only marginally affected by economic sanctions, or for those convicted of currency crimes, which were considered in eighteenth-century Massachusetts as a threat to the security of the government. Martha Edwards was sentenced to one year of imprisonment without "Bail or Mainprize" for counterfeiting.[13] The court was very careful to make the distinction between routine jailing during trial proceedings, for which a defendant could seek bail, and incarceration, for which the accused could not gain release. Mercy Maker was another currency violator. The Harwich spinster was sentenced to two years at hard labor in the house of correction for uttering counterfeit bills of credit in 1771.[14] Lesser terms of imprisonment were handed down by the justices as well. A three-month sentence was given to Boston spinster Margaret Johnson in 1766 for assaulting Catherine Neal, an "infant."[15] Margaret Read pleaded guilty to assault and theft against William Pitman's daughter, Elizabeth, in 1723 and was sentenced to thirty days in the house of correction "to receive the discipline of the house."[16] Only nine women were sentenced to a term of imprisonment; four of these spent only thirty days in jail, three were incarcerated up to six months in the house of correction, and only two were sentenced to a year or more in prison. These were sentences of incarceration, not terms spent in county jails before trial or while awaiting sentence.

If the least frequent punishment was incarceration, the

most frequent was whipping. Public flogging was a versatile form of punishment that was not dependent on the economic capacity of the prisoner, and its severity could be easily controlled to fit the crime and circumstances. Ten stripes were the minimum, and the number could be increased gradually to twenty or thirty up to the maximum that was considered not life-threatening, thirty-nine. Both Sabina and Coffee, the two black slaves transported, also suffered thirty-nine stripes before being shipped from the colony. Most often those sentenced to being whipped were given the middle range of lashes. Elizabeth Smith, a "singlewoman" of Boston, was twice sentenced to receive twenty stripes for her two convictions for felonious stealing in the 1770s.[17] The limitation of thirty-nine stripes could be exceeded in a case that the justices thought was extremely severe. As in the case of Anna, a Negro, the bench prescribed that thirty stripes be given immediately and then required her to spend a month in prison, recuperating, after which she was again whipped thirty stripes, for a total of sixty.[18] Forty women suffered whippings as sentences from the high courts. Ten received ten stripes or less, sixteen got twenty stripes or less, three suffered between twenty-one and thirty stripes, and eleven women faced thirty-one or more lashes.

The court did not intend that the prisoners sentenced to whippings suffer permanent damage or death. If there was any question as to the physical condition of the convicted woman, the sentence was deferred, as it was for Anne Grafton. Grafton was convicted in August 1748 of three counts of felonious stealing from two merchants and a distiller in Boston but was not given her three whippings of ten stripes each until a year later, "she being then in a weak and distemper'd condition the court did not proceed to pass sentence against her but respited the same until this term."[19] A whipping would also be delayed when a woman was pregnant. For Margret Lampsen, convicted of adultery in 1758, the sentence of ten stripes was delayed for four months, after a jury of matrons determined that she was seven months pregnant.[20]

Next to execution, the most severe and permanent sanction a felon could face in early Massachusetts was mutilation. Most often this was applied in felony cases in which the accused was convicted of a second offense. Only six women were so punished. Mutilation varied in type and severity, from the branding of a "B" on the forehead of a convicted burglar, such as free black woman Lucy Little in 1772, to the cutting off an ear of a counterfeiter, as was done to widow Martha Edwards of Boston in 1723.[21] Mutilation was also used as a mitigation of a clergyable capital offense, as in the case of Sarah Forland's bigamy conviction in 1756. The king's attorney asked for the death penalty, but Forland asked for benefit of clergy and was granted it; she was summarily burned in the hand.[22] Katherine Hartnon was also given benefit of clergy in 1687 for breaking and entering the house of Daniell Mathews of Boston and stealing 5s. 8d., whereupon the letter "T" was burned in her hand.[23] That same year Mercy Windsor was granted benefit of clergy by the court and had the letter "T" burned in her hand for felonious stealing.[24] A total of five women were granted benefit of clergy by the high courts.

There were miscellaneous other punishments given out by the court, usually in conjunction with one or more of the above. Twenty-four women's sentences included one of these. One of the most common additional penalties was to be required to stand on the gallows with a rope around the neck. Several convicted adulterers were so sentenced, including Hannah Parker of Plymouth in 1707, Jemima Colefix of Boston in 1721, and Mary Rainer of Sheffield in 1752.[25] These women, like Nathaniel Hawthorne's Hester Prynne, were also required to wear forever a capital "A," in different colored cloths. Each time they were found without their letter, they could be subject to a whipping of fifteen stripes. The requirement to wear a permanent letter was not a relic of early seventeenth-century Puritanism, for it persisted as a legitimate punishment well into the eighteenth century. Nor was the "A" for adultery the only letter prescribed by the justices. Eunice Clefson, a single woman of Deerfield, was convicted of incest in 1756 with her brother-in-law, Joseph Severance, and was sentenced to perpetually wear a letter "I."[26] Three years later Huldah Dudley of Concord faced the same punishment for "Voluntarily, Incestuously and Adulterously" sleeping with her stepfather, Judah Clark.[27] The pillory was still being used in the eighteenth century as well. Mary Richards spent two hours locked in the pillory for fraud in 1750, and Meriam Fitch spent one hour in the pillory with the words A CHEAT pinned on her breast.[28]

The most severe punishment in colonial Massachusetts was execution. Nineteen women were hanged between the years 1673 and 1774. Elizabeth Emmerson and her parents John and Esther were sentenced to death for the murder of her newborn bastard twins in 1693.[29] Three years later Susanna Andrews, also convicted of infanticide of bastard twins, was hanged.[30] Hannah Degoe, a mulatto woman of Reheboth, was sentenced to death by the court in 1710 for the murder of her bastard.[31] A Falmouth Indian named Patience was punished with death for the murder of her neighbor's son.[32] One of the few women hanged in this period for an offense other than murder was Mary Rogers, a woman of many aliases and an incorrigible thief. After her burglary conviction in 1749, she was sentenced to death.[33]

Not all women convicted of capital offenses were hanged. Of the thirty-eight female defendants found guilty of capital crimes, nineteen were hanged, seventeen were punished by a sanction other than death, and two did not have their punishment recorded. These women were spared by benefit of clergy, a reduction of the charge, or a "special verdict." The first of these was provided by law and did not involve the discretion of the court. There was, however, no benefit of clergy for murder; of the seventeen defendants who escaped execution, seven were charged with murder. In their cases the charge was reduced to homicidal negligence, manslaughter, or a similar non-capital offense, so that conviction would not require the death penalty. It is not clear who was responsible for the reduction of charge. The king's attorney could ask for a lesser charge, or a jury could bring in a verdict of guilty upon a lesser charge, but the key role was played by the judges. We know that they took an active role at the trial. They interviewed jurors, questioned witnesses, and instructed all concerned on the law. They even theoretically protected the rights of the accused at the trial.[34] Special verdicts were actually queries directed to the bench by the jury. In 1758 jurors told the justices that they would find Flora guilty of infanticide, under the Stuart statute of 1624, if she was declared to be single. If the justices credited her claims to be married to a fellow slave, the child would not be a bastard, and the statute would not apply. In such event the jury would find insufficient evidence of murder (only concealment of the corpse was proven) and so vote to acquit. Flora went free when the justices accepted her marriage claim.[35]

How did the court decide who should live or die? As John Kaplan has written, it is in the area of sentencing "that we must grapple most with the judge's discretion."[36] John Hogarth has approached the problem of judges' discretion by studying the socioeconomic background and attitudes of the justices themselves.[37] It is not possible to do this for the colonial Massachusetts high court bench, but evidence does indicate that the judges' views of crime and criminals were not very different from the segment of society that made up the juries. If anything, the Sewalls, Lyndes, and Winthrops on the court, not to mention the Stoughtons, were religiously conventional and socially conservative.[38] Samuel Sewall, usually reticent in his diary about his reactions to verdicts in his court, expressed strong disapproval of Esther Rogers on the occasion of her sentencing: "I told her that God had put two Children in her to nurse: Her Mother did not serve her so. Esther was a great saviour; she, a great destroyer." He justified this uncharacteristic outburst by claiming that he "did not do this to insult over her, but to make her sensible."[39] The opinions of Thomas Hutchinson on the severity of sentences for offenders against the social order were succinctly expressed in his 1768 charge to the grand jury. He denounced the conduct of the younger generation of rabblerousers and mobs, from which he would later particularly suffer, and suggested capital punishment as a fitting solution to youthful disobedience.[40] If the judges shared the biases and expectations of antifeminism, the same variables that could have potentially influenced conviction should reappear in sentencing. That is, the same prejudices that jurors might have showed in reaching a verdict should also exist in the judges' sentence.

The first telling characteristics for discretion in sentencing and punishment of females was the race of the accused. Table 14 shows the variation in this category. White women con-

TABLE 14. Execution of Sentence by Race of Accused

| | | Race of Accused | | | |
		White	Black	Indian	Row Total
	Unknown	2 [7.1]	0	0	0 [5.3]
Execution of Sentence	Yes	12 (63.2) [42.9]	6 (31.6) [66.7]	1 (5.3) [100.0]	19 [50.0]
	No	14 (82.4) [50.0]	3 (17.6) [33.3]	0	17 [44.7]

Note. Numbers in parentheses indicate *row* percentage; in brackets, *column* percentages.

victed of capital crimes had a slightly greater chance to avoid execution than black women, who were executed two-thirds of the time. The sole Indian woman convicted by the court was sentenced to die. The court was harsher toward minorities than whites in its application of the death penalty.

The next variable that might influence sentencing discretion was the venue of the trial. Did the county in which the court met also have an effect on the proportion of convicted women who faced the death penalty? There was variation in the percentage of women sentenced to die from county to county. Suffolk, which had the largest number of women at risk to suffer death, had the lowest percentage of those actually condemned, 38.9 percent. Essex had a higher proportion, 40 percent; Middlesex was yet higher, at 60 percent. Plymouth women convicted of capital crimes inevitably were hanged; all four women convicted in that county were executed. This variation in the geography of execution can be partly explained by the types of crimes that were heard in the counties. Women convicted of murder were least likely to escape: fifteen of the nineteen hanged were murderers. These offenses were distributed throughout all the counties. The property and morals offenders convicted but not executed were concentrated in the counties of Suffolk, Essex, and Middlesex.

The last variable discussed in the earlier stages of the criminal trial was the sex of the suspect. Recent scholarship has proposed two opposing theories for the relationship between gender and sentencing. The paternalistic theory suggests that women suffered less severe punishments than men for similar crimes. William J. Hockhammer cites studies of twentieth-century capital punishment that show this discrimination. "For example, even though women commit about one of every seven murders, of the 3,298 people executed for murder from 1930 through 1962, only thirty were women."[41] Freda Adler and Rita James Simon express the theory more generally: "when male judges are confronted by a female defendant (so the argument has been stated) it is difficult for them not to imagine their own mothers, sisters, or wives in the same circumstances, and act accordingly."[42] Though this model has fallen into some disrepute in recent years and, even if valid, its effects have been reduced since the women's movement of the 1960s and 1970s, it could still be valid for eighteenth-century justices.

The second theory is the disfavored model. The presumption here is that a woman is treated more harshly than a man at the sentencing stage "because [judges] see in her behavior a greater discrepancy between the behavior expected of a woman and her actual behavior than they do between the behavior expected of a man and the actual behavior of a male defendant."[43] The prime evidence for this model is found in how county and church courts handle immorality cases. Rarely does one see it in the Superior Court of Judicature. The case of Hannah and David Moore of Worcester, convicted of assaulting Jemima Lovell, may be one (though as an assault, it could have been brought in the lower court). Hannah was fined £3 while David was fined only 30s. Perhaps Hannah started the fray, or the court may have been harsher on Hannah because they disapproved of violence in women more than men. David may have been her son, and she may have been held responsible for his part in the incident, although we know from the indictment that David Moore was not identified as an infant; his occupation was given as laborer. The difference between their sentences could very well have been a reproof against Hannah for behavior particularly unbecoming for a woman, while David might have been less severely punished for only acting like other men.[44]

To compare men's and women's sentencing patterns, we must limit ourselves to those crimes for which they would be susceptible to the same punishment and which were closely similar by type to one another. Thus, we limit ourselves to defendants convicted of capital offenses. As we have seen, thirty-eight women were convicted of capital crimes; 100 men were likewise found guilty. Fifty percent of the women were sentenced to death, compared with 54 percent of the men. The men did face execution slightly more often than women. The lack of variation between men's and women's sentences might mask differences in the characteristics of those condemned, and tests for this possibility are easily arranged.

The first variation in the sentencing of men and women for capital crimes may be in the types of crimes that were committed. As we have seen, women almost invariably suffered death for homicide: 78.9 percent were so judged. Men were hanged for homicide at very nearly the same proportion: 79.6 percent. This is not surprising, since premeditated homicide is a *mala in se* crime, condemned throughout society, and the one most often to meet with society's most severe reprisals. The other crime categories have nearly identical percentages for men and women with the exception of the "Other Personal" category. In this category 75 percent of the women charged and ultimately convicted escaped the death sentence; men only avoided death in this crime category 54.5 percent of the time. Of the eleven men convicted in this group, ten were originally charged with rape, a serious and ancient felony that only applied to men. Three of the eleven had the rape charge reduced to assault with intent to rape. The remaining suspects were sentenced to death, and three were hanged. When rape convictions are removed from the picture, men and women appear to have been treated equally well in the sentencing process, regardless of the type of crimes they committed.

A second characteristic that affected execution rates was race. Minority women had a disproportionate number of death sentences. Was this pattern the same for men? White men had close to the same percentage of death sentences as white women, 46.3 percent to 42.9 percent. Though the men had a slightly higher likelihood of execution, the majority of white men, like women, avoided hanging. Male blacks fared less well; they were condemned in proportions similar to black women, not white men. Black men were hanged in 68.8 percent of their cases. Male Indians did not escape punishment, as they had convictions: slightly more than 70 percent of Indian men were executed after being charged with a capital crime. The single Indian woman convicted was also hanged. The difficulties in convicting Indians—lack of evidence, unwillingness of witnesses to testify, and ease of concealment of crimes—were gone once the verdict was rendered. Even more than the guilty black, the Indian convicted of homicide (for all these cases were homicides) was dealt with severely.

The final variable that might affect the difference between male and female executions was the gender of the victims. For women this played no part in their sentences. The percentage of execution for women who committed crimes against females was almost identical with those whose crimes were against males. The discrimination against women committing intersexual crimes had been made at the time of indictment and conviction. This conclusion holds true for male defendants, too. There was no significant difference in the execution or relief of men from the death penalty on the basis of the gender of their victim ($Q = .099$).[45]

If the characteristics of defendants and their victims had little or no effect on the passing of the death penalty, there is yet one possible variable that could have affected this sentence: the circumstances of the court proceedings themselves. In the Friends Service Committee's *Struggle for Justice: A Report on Crime and Punishment in America* (1971), the original plea of the defendants to the charge laid against them was found to affect the severity of the sentence prescribed by the justices. A defendant who pleaded guilty suffered a lighter sentence than one who put the court to the trouble and expense of a jury trial. The study concluded that "there is a close correlation between type of plea and type and length of punishment."[46] This mechanism was also at work in the eighteenth century. Defendants who put themselves "upon court and country" and pleaded innocence might, if convicted, still be able to obtain a reduction of charge and, with it, a reduction of sentence. Even so, those who pleaded guilty to the full extent of the charges against them were treated more mercifully than those who pleaded not guilty. (This did not affect capital offenses for women, for reasons that will be discussed shortly.) It did affect sentences for less serious offenses, as illustrated by the distribution of stripes at the whipping post shown in Table 15. The effect of the type of plea upon the severity of corporal punishment is clearly evident. At every increment in the number of stripes, women who had pleaded not guilty received a considerably higher percentage than those who had not contended the charge. The severity of punishment for those convicted of lesser felonies was mitigated by the plea of guilty. (In capital trials the plea of guilty could have only a limited effect on sentence, for the latter was determined by whether the law left room for mercy.)

TABLE 15. Distribution of Stripes by Plea of the Defendant

		Plea		Row Total
		Guilty	Not Guilty	
	1–10	2 (25%)	6 (75%)	8
Number of Stripes	11–20	5 (35.7%)	9 (64.3%)	14
	21–30	0 (0)	3 (100.0%)	3
	31+	1 (12.5%)	7 (87.5%)	8
	Column total	8 (24.2%)	25 (75.8%)	33

Note. The numbers in parentheses indicate *row* percentages.

To summarize, personal characteristics, except for race, had little appreciable effect on the sentence of accused women. Certain procedures within the trial itself could affect the punishment meted out to women guilty of lesser felonies: reduction of the original charge to one requiring less severe punishment by statute, and the reduction of punishment by the judge after a plea of guilty. The limited role of discretion in the area of punishment can be explained in part as a result of the application of discretion at indictment and trial. It is also true that the court recognized that punishment had another purpose, in the face of which the defendants' characteristics claimed secondary attention.

At this last stage of the criminal process the court no longer focused solely upon the individual defendant but upon the offense—and all offenses like it. Punishment became an expression of community censure, and the defendant a symbol of disorder, violence, and sin. In this setting the extent of discretion was sharply curtailed deliberately. Certainly the limitations that statute and code placed upon punishments had something to do with the relative uniformity of punishment. Punishment was far better defined in the colonial law than the use of evidence or the burden of proof, concepts involved in indicting and convicting a suspect. But the absence of discretion was not a by-product of the law; it was a major function of the entire system. In every society punishment goes beyond the individual convict to teach a lesson to the people. This lesson is meant for men and women who might become criminals themselves and for those who wish to see concrete evidence that wrongdoers are paying for their crimes. Both pronouncement of sentence and administration of punishment were surrounded with rituals to reassure the community that crime was being repaid and to warn the would-be criminal. For this reason, judges attempted to mete out sentences that did not take away from the solemnity or the fairness of the entire proceedings and expressed the inevitability of punishment for those condemned by the community.

Punishment is the most visible proof of the efficacy of the justice system. While capture, indictment, and pretrial procedures were almost hidden, the conviction and punishment of criminals were, in these centuries, open to the public. Only a few men and women could crowd into the courts to hear the sentence spoken, but many could and did attend the punishments.

As Samuel Sewall noted in his diary on the occasion of Cotton Mather's execution sermon for Sarah Threeneedles, the South Meetinghouse was filled with "a very vast Assembly, and the street full of such as could not get in."[47] Cotton Mather, in his diary, remarked on the same event that at the lecture "the greatest Assembly, ever in this country preached unto, was now come together; it may be four or five thousand Souls. I could not get unto the *Pulpit,* but by climbing over *Pues* and *Heads.*"[48] The large crowds were not merely incident to the spectacle, but they were an encouraged necessity. The sermons of Mather or Benjamin Colman, though ostensibly addressed to the culprit, were really meant for the public at large. Michel Foucault agrees that "in the ceremonies of the public execution, the main character was the people, whose real and immediate presence was required for the performance."[49] When Mather described the spectacle of the Threeneedles's lecture, he admitted that on the day of the lecture he had felt "weak," "faint," and "spent," but after climbing to his pulpit and seeing the multitudes that came to hear him preach, "the Spirit of my dearest Lord came upon me. I preached with a more than ordinary Assistance, and enlarged, and uttered the most awakening things, for near two Hours together."[50]

From the courtroom to the meetinghouse to the gallows, officials, justices, ministers, prisoner, and crowd marched. The message of the pain and shame of punishment was visible to all. The public spectacle continued at the pillory and the gallows. Sewall saw evidence of public shaming and the crowd's participation in the event on a trip to London as a young man and noted it in his diary with no surprise: "This day two stood in the Pillory before the Royal Exchange. . . . They were exceedingly pelted with dirt and Eggs."[51] The Massachusetts crowds might arguably have been more decorous, yet it is not hard to imagine what the reaction of the populace on lecture day might have been at the sight of Abigail Johnson, in 1677, standing on the gallows with a rope around her neck, then tied to the cartstail, stripped to the waist and whipped.[52] Nor is it hard to envision the public response to seeing Meriam Fitch and her accomplice standing on the pillory for an hour with the words A CHEAT on their breasts.[53]

The women who went to the gallows did so in such a way as to involve the public's participation. The crowds at Sarah Threeneedles's execution could hardly have missed the spectacle produced at noon on lecture day. Nor was Threeneedles an exception; the time for these events was invariably set for the middle of the day. No one thought of scheduling hangings for early morning hours, as they did in a later, more private era. Mary Rogers met her maker sometime between three and five in the afternoon.[54] Elizabeth Colson was hanged between noon and 5:00 P.M.[55] Esther Rogers was hanged between 10 A.M. and 5 P.M. on "a gibbet in Ipswich at Pyngrass Plain."[56] All of the condemned met with their fate in the middle of the day or early afternoon, after the dire public sermons of the ministers.

The messages of the ministers combined both retributive and deterrent elements.[57] Robert Bosco, analyzing the Puritan execution sermons, concluded that they were an exhortation on God's wrath directed to the whole community—a warning that the sinfulness Puritans knew lurked in every heart must be scourged.[58] The message of the sermons went beyond this warning that sinful conduct would be met with retribution. Ministers exhorted, and the execution rituals displayed a message of deterrence. This theme is clear in the words of the Reverend Charles Chauncy: " '[It] is capable of wise use, and you may receive lasting advantage' from 'the tragical end of this unhappy criminal.' "[59] In 1771 Moses Baldwin "told an execution audience to behave themselves 'with all decency and moderation, [and] to stand off from everything rude and vain,' lest they too become spectacles at the scaffold."[60]

The punishment of women played a special part in this dual expression of repentance and deterrence, for women were the most vulnerable of those who might be punished. With children, they were "protected" by the laws. The sight of a woman at the whipping post or the gallows must have been a moving one. Even the most hardened of female criminals became a pitiable object when punishment was given her. Her shame and pain were especially cathartic to the multitude, arousing a sympathetic chord of suffering. In her punishment they could feel the lash or the noose and be purified of sin—at least for a moment. At the same time the ministers' narratives of women's careers in crime offered vivid lessons in the road to ruin. Women were urged, even on the gallows, to confess their sins that others might be deterred from the same path. Mather and others disseminated these confessions.[61] Of the eighteen execution sermons published in the heyday of this genre, between 1690 and 1720, seven concerned women, a number far exceeding their proportion of the total of persons executed.

Women were important symbols in the effort to deter crime because the crimes of women could be traced back to sexual breaches. Once they had "fallen" into the snares of "lust" and "uncleanness," they were ripe for thefts, homicides, and arsons.[62] Women sentenced for crime thereby became a symbol, a living border of sexual deviance. As we have seen, Puritan society was concerned about the issue of sexual deviance from the inception of the movement in sixteenth-century England. The female criminal, because of her gender, became an appropriate target for these concerns. Since many female crimes did have a real sexual aspect—infanticides and adulteries in particular—the use of female criminals to teach lessons of continence and modesty to the young women of the colony seemed to make eminent sense.

With the waning of Puritanism, and the changing condition of women's lives and of attitudes toward women in the eighteenth century, women's role as symbols of deviance disappeared. A striking shift in the sentencing of women over time demonstrates this revolution (Table 16). Women were charged far more frequently with capital offenses in the seventeenth century than in the next seventy-four years, but many more of them escaped execution in the 1600s than in the 1700s by a reduction of the charge. In the seventeenth

TABLE 16. A Comparison between the Seventeenth and Eighteenth Centuries in the Number of Women Originally Charged with Capital Offenses, Convicted, and Condemned to Death

| | | Century | | Row Total |
		17th (1673–99)	18th (1700–1774)	
Death Penalty	Yes	6	12	18
	No	13	4	17
	Column Total	19	16	35

Note. $Q = .733$, and $\phi = -.629$.

century the symbolic form was preserved, as the trial of these women played out its course, but culpability was obviously not established in the judges' or jurors' minds. The eighteenth century saw fewer women charged with capital offenses, and fewer convictions, but those convicted were hanged. Of the sixteen women convicted of capital offenses, all but four received the prescribed penalty of death. These women were not tried and symbolically punished on weak cases for the edification of the populace. The growing liberation of women in the courts brought with it a bittersweet conclusion.

NOTES

1. Fitch's case, SCJ 1763–64, 11–12 (Jan. 25, 1763).
2. Richards's case, SCJ 1747–50, 367–68 (Mar. 18, 1750).
3. Young's case, SCJ 1766–67, 109–10 (Aug. 6, 1762).
4. Waters's case, SCJ 1763–64, 133 (Aug. 16, 1763).
5. Sabina's case, SCJ 3:238 (May 4, 1709).
6. Terry's case, SCJ 1743–47, 33 (Aug. 16, 1743).
7. Trefy's case, SCJ 1766–67, 266–67 (June 19, 1767).
8. Shepard's case, SCJ 2:45–46 (Jan. 28, 1696).
9. Bushell's case, SCJ 1747–50, 86–87 (Feb. 16, 1748).
10. Coffee's case, SCJ 3:288–89 (Sept. 12, 1713).
11. On the flow of convicts to the New World, see Abbott E. Smith, *Colonists in Bondage,* rev. ed. (New York, 1971 [orig. publ. 1941]), especially 316–17. Few of these convicts came to New England.
12. David Rothman, *The Discovery of the Asylum: Social Order and Disorder in the New Republic* (Boston, 1971), 48, argues that confinement was not normal until the nineteenth century. While the precise timing of the introduction of long jail terms as specific punishments (not due to delays in trial and/or sentencing) is uncertain, the shift to punishing male criminals with jail terms was well underway by the end of the Revolution, as corporal punishment, shaming, and binding out in servitude lost effectiveness. See Adam J. Hirsch, "From Pillory to Penitentiary: The Rise of Criminal Incarceration in Early Massachusetts," *Michigan Law Review* 80 (1982), 1231.
13. Edwards's case, SCJ 1721–25, 120 (May 7, 1723).
14. Maker's case, SCJ 1771, 44 (May 1771).
15. Johnson's case, SCJ 1766–67, 109–10 (Aug. 26, 1766).
16. Read's case, SCJ 1721–25, 162–63 (Nov. 5, 1723).
17. Smith's case, SCJ 1771, 41 (Feb. 19, 1771); SCJ 1772, 39 (Feb. 18, 1772–Mar. 10, 1772).
18. Anna's case, *Court of Assistants,* 1:29–30 (Mar. 2, 1674).
19. Grafton's case, SCJ 1747–50, 275 (Aug. 15, 1749).
20. Lampsen's case, SCJ 1757–59, 391–92 (Aug. 1, 1758).

21. Little's case, SCJ 1772, 122–23 (Aug. 25, 1772); Edwards's case, SCJ 1721–25, 120 (May 7, 1723).

22. Forland's case, SCJ 1755–56, 222–23 (Feb. 17, 1756). On benefit of clergy, see page 00, above.

23. Hartnon's case, SCJ 1:18 (Apr. 26, 1687).

24. Windsor's case, SCJ 1:19 (Apr. 26, 1687).

25. Parker's case, SCJ 3:206 (Mar. 27, 1707); Colefix's case, SCJ 1715–21, 355–56 (May 2, 1721); Rainer's case, SCJ 1752–53, 190 (Sept. 26, 1752).

26. Clefson (Clesson)'s case, SCJ 1755–56, 341–42 (Sept. 20, 1756).

27. Dudley's case, SCJ 1757–59, 655 (Aug. 7, 1759).

28. Richards's case, SCJ 1747–50, 367–68 (Mar. 18, 1750); Fitch's case, SCJ 1763–64, 11–12 (Jan. 25, 1763).

29. Emmerson's case, SCJ 1:50–51 (Apr. 25, 1693).

30. Andrew's case, SCJ 2:49–50 (Mar. 10, 1696).

31. Degoe's case, SCJ 3:253 (Sept. 12, 1710).

32. Patience's case, SCJ 1733–36, 228 (June 18, 1735).

33. Mary Rogers's case, SCJ 1747–50, 188 (Jan. 31, 1749).

34. On the role of the judges, see John H. Langbein, "The Criminal Trial before the Lawyers," *University of Chicago Law Review* 45 (Winter 1978), 263–316.

35. Flora's case, SCJ 1757–59, 295–96 (Feb. 21, 1758).

36. John Kaplan, *Criminal Justice: Introductory Cases and Materials,* 2d ed. (Mineola, N.Y., 1978), 455.

37. John Hogarth, *Sentencing as a Human Process* (Toronto, 1971), 15–33.

38. A collective biography of the justices on the court would be out of place here, but it can be said that they were religiously and socially conservative. See, for example, the diaries left by Sewall, quoted below, as well as Richard S. Dunn, *Puritans and Yankees: The Winthrop Dynasty of New England, 1630–1717* (New York, 1971), on Wait Winthrop; the sketch of William Stoughton in *Biographical Sketches of Those Who Attended Harvard College* (Boston, 1873); Bernard Bailyn, *The Ordeal of Thomas Hutchinson* (Cambridge, Mass., 1974), on Hutchinson; and the introduction to *Peter Oliver's Origin and Progress of the American Rebellion,* ed. Douglass Adair and John Schutz (San Marino, Calif., 1970), on the last royal chief justice.

39. *The Diary of Samuel Sewall, 1674–1729,* ed. M. Halsey Thomas (New York, 1972), 1:451.

40. Thomas Hutchinson to the Suffolk grand jury, March 1768, quoted in *Reports of Cases . . . Taken By Josiah Quincy, Jr.,* ed. Samuel Quincy (Boston, 1856), 259.

41. William J. Hockhammer, "The Capital Punishment Controversy," in *Crime and Justice,* ed. Jerome H. Skolnick et al. (Del Mar, Calif., 1977), 164.

42. Freda Adler and Rita James Simon, eds., *The Criminology of Deviant Women* (Boston, 1979), 250.

43. Adler and Simon, eds., *Deviant Women,* 250.

44. Moore's case, SCJ 1757–59, 715 (Sept. 18, 1759).

45. Edward Green, "Inter- and Intra-Racial Crime Relative to Sentencing," in *Race, Crime, and Justice*, ed. Charles E. Reasons and Jack L. Kuykendall (Pacific Palisades, Calif., 1972), 284–99, argues that the sentencing stage is the least susceptible to racial prejudice today.

46. American Friends Service Committee, *Struggle for Justice: A Report on Crime and Punishment in America* (New York, 1971), 139.

47. *Diary of Sewall*, 1:400.

48. *The Diary of Cotton Mather*, ed. Worthington C. Ford (New York, 1911–12), Nov. 17, 1698.

49. Michel Foucault, *Discipline and Punish: The Birth of the Prison*, trans. Alan Sheridan (New York, 1977), 57.

50. Mather, *Diary*, Nov. 17, 1698.

51. *Diary of Sewall*, 1:227.

52. The impact of the rituals of punishment depended on empathy, and support for the authorities mingled with sympathy for the accused. See Michael Ignatieff, *A Just Measure of Pain* (New York, 1978), 21.

53. See Hawthorne's imaginative reconstruction of these feelings in the first powerful chapter of the *Scarlet Letter* (1851).

54. Mary Rogers's case, SCJ 1747–50, 188 (Jan. 31, 1749).

55. Colson's case, SCJ 1725–29, 111 (Apr. 25, 1727).

56. Esther Rogers's case, SCJ 3:49 (July 15, 1701).

57. The "retributive" and the "deterrent" theories of punishment are distinct, but may be blended in any particular culture. The deterrent theory is that punishment must "prevent crime"; see Ernest van den Haag, *Punishing Criminals* (New York, 1975), 156. The retributive theory is well expressed in biblical literature: an eye for an eye.

58. Robert Bosco, "Lectures at the Pillory: The Early American Execution Sermon," *American Quarterly* 30 (Summer 1978), 156–76.

59. Charles Chauncy, *The Horrid Nature and Enormous Guilt of Murder* (Boston, 1754), 22.

60. Moses Baldwin, *The Ungodly Condemned in Judgment* (Boston, 1771), 24.

61. See Mather, *Pillars of Salt* (Boston, 1699), passim.

62. This objective did not disappear with the decline in sex-related offenses; see Bosco, "Lectures," 175–76.

CHAPTER SEVEN

WOMEN'S SERIOUS CRIMES
IN RETROSPECT AND PROSPECT

Over the past decade law enforcement authorities, followed by the popular media, have warned about a wave of serious crime. The phenomenon, going back to the end of World War II, reverses the trend of a century and a half in England and America. It appears that women offenders are playing a major part in this crime wave, a fact disturbing in itself but even more potentially damaging to the women's liberation movement. If crime levels are related to opportunity levels, wider participation of women in the world of business and larger numbers of women working outside the home may be tied directly to the increasing number of women charged with serious crimes. It is undeniably true that a larger proportion of serious crimes are being committed by women: from 1953 through 1972, the percentage of women arrested for serious crimes rose from 9.4 percent to 19.25 percent.[1] The increase came primarily in the category of crimes against property, which can be considered the by-products of the freedom to work and live in public. The ratio of female participation in the commission of crimes against the person has not changed nearly as much between 1953 and 1972. When women do commit crimes against property, they are far more likely to act as conspirators, accessories, or partners with men than to act alone.[2] In crimes against the person the reverse is true. In homicides and assaults (for which there is a very similar pattern of data) women are three times more likely to act alone than in concert with anyone else. Their victims are their children, husbands, and lovers, the majority of whom are helpless when the attack occurs. Violent crimes by women remain impulsive responses to particular situations; they appear to be unaffected by the reform of women's place in society.

Are these conclusions, so controversial today, substantiated by historical data? The missing statistical component in modern studies is the data that historians are perfectly placed to provide: changing rates over time. Let us reexamine Massachusetts colonial society and economy in the eighteenth century. It was a time of modernization and growing materialism, with citizens frustrated by periodic bouts of depressed prices, unbalanced budgets, and unemployment. War disclocated the normal channels of trade three times in the century. Despite these troubles, women gradually found their way to a larger role in their communities—if only during wartime. Though their activities seem small by comparison with their sphere today, women moved about more freely in the marketplace and business streets at the end of the colonial era than at its inception. Freedom of movement brought opportunity for crime as well as legal exchanges of services. Then, as now, women worked with men to commit crimes against property. When men's participation in crimes against property fell, due to the wars against France, women's crimes against property also declined drastically. Because these crimes were so closely tied to specific opportunities and to immediate external conditions, their numbers were much more variable than crimes against persons, a pattern apparent in the figures in Chapter 3. (See Appendix 3 as well.) Thus far, the historical record seems to support explanations of recent data.[3]

Crimes against the person are a more complicated subject than crimes against property for the modern criminologist and the historian of crime. They have a more complex etiology, combining external opportunity with passionate motives absent from crimes against property. One expects, all else being equal, that modern societies will have lower rates of crime against the person than premodern societies. Theory claims that as we grow sophisticated, we grow to care more about ourselves and others. From the time we are born in a modern society, we are taught how to get along with others. Violence is sublimated into games and careers. Life becomes more precious. Only in subcultures of violence—certain bars in certain districts of town, certain "mean streets"—is violence still acceptable as a way of preserving honor. Women's serious crimes against the person, though never approaching the number of men's homicides and assaults, should also decline as society becomes more modern, and historically this seems to be so. In the thirteenth century selected English eyre and assize court records show between 37.8 and 13.6 murders and manslaughters per 100,000 adults (though the full legal distinction was not made between them until the sixteenth century). James Given argues either that many more cases went unreported or that for some reported cases, no one was indicted in the courts. Women's part in this can be estimated. Some 8.6 percent of all Given's thirteenth-century suspects were female.[4] By the end of the sixteenth century and the beginning of the seventeenth century, these figures had declined. Late Elizabethan Essex had but 4.9 murders and manslaughters tried in the courts per year in an adult population of perhaps 40,000, or 12.3 indictments per 100,000 adults.[5] The murder indictment rates for Middlesex, including London, in the period 1613–18, were 17.0 per 100,000 adults, and 32 percent of these cases had at least one female suspect.[6] Figure 3 in Chapter 3 presents decadal rates of indictments for males and females in eighteenth-century Massachusetts; these are lower than the comparable rates for Middlesex and London in the seventeenth century. Indeed, even the teeming metropolis, though a center of crime in England, saw a decline in indictments for all violent crimes, to a rate of 26.2 per 100,000 adults by the mid-eighteenth century.[7]

These figures can be compared with modern crime rates. The U.S. Department of Justice collects annual homicide arrest statistics from almost all of the police departments in the country. These are not the same as indictment figures, for not every arrest leads to an indictment. All else being equal, arrest figures should be considerably in excess of the indictment figures. For the period between 1968 and 1981, these arrest figures are given in Table 17. The difference between arrests and indictments can be estimated. In 1969 only 817 men and women were charged by grand juries with murder or manslaughter.[8] This is but 5.5 percent of those arrested. In 1972, 1,016 men and women were charged in court for these offenses—5.4 percent of those arrested. If this 5.5 percentage ratio is close to correct, then the arrest rate must be multiplied by 0.055 to get an indictment rate comparable to the one I have employed for the eighteenth-century court records. Multiplying the female twentieth-century arrest rates in this way gives an average indictment rate of 0.146 (2.66 × .055) per 100,000 adult females. This modern indictment rate is one-tenth of the eighteenth-century rate.

TABLE 17. Arrests and Arrest Rates for Murder and Non-Negligent Manslaughter, by Age and Sex, in the United States, 1968–81

Year	Arrest Total	Female Arrests	Arrest Rate/ 100,000 Adult[a] Females[b]
1968	10,394	1,672	2.27
1969	11,509	1,746	2.33
1970	12,836	1,979	2.60
1971	14,549	2,365	3.05
1972	15,049	2,322	2.94
1973	14,399	2,176	2.71
1974	13,818	2,018	2.47
1975	16,485	2,573	3.10
1976	14,113	2,102	2.43
1977	17,163	2,493	2.84
1978	18,755	2,652	2.98
1979	18,264	2,503	2.71
1980	18,745	2,391	2.56
1981	20,432	2,586	2.73

SOURCE. U.S. Department of Justice, *Crime in the United States: Uniform Crime Reports* (Washington, D.C., 1968–81).
[a]Adults are defined as persons over fourteen years of age.
[b]The population figures are from the U.S. Department of Commerce, Bureau of the Census, *Population Estimates and Projections* (Washington, D.C., 1972–82).

From the colonial period to the present, women have followed the course prescribed for them by modernization theory, and this trend is evident in colonial Massachusetts. Figure 7 shows that the rate at which women were prosecuted for homicides declined drastically ($R^2 = .758$), even as the number of women who could be charged with these crimes (that is, adults) increased tremendously. One crucial factor in this decline was

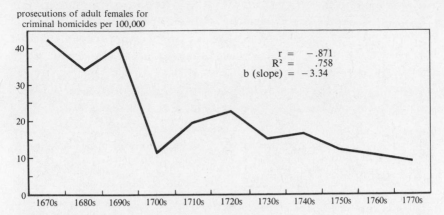

FIGURE 7. Adult Female Rate for Criminal Homicide, per 100,000, in Massachusetts, 1670–1779

the decrease in infanticide, a shift in female behavior that has been linked to modernization.[9] Rates for other offenses were also declining during these decades (see Chapter 3), so that the homicide figures confirm larger trends continuing through the next century.[10] If the rate of women's homicide strongly follows the path predicted by modernization theory ($R^2 = .758$), declining steeply with the passage of time ($\beta = -3.34$)—as is the case with other types of serious crimes in this era—the ratio of women's criminal homicides to men's does not support this theory. With increasing equality of movement and opportunity, women should have been increasing their share of these crimes. They did not.

Graphs of both the percentage of female criminal homicides of the total number of cases (using the case as a denominator; see Figure 7) and of the total number of defendants (using the actual number of individuals indicted for the cases as the denominator; see Figure 8) show that women's participation in these crimes did not increase. There is no trend in either of these graphs ($r = -.195$; and $r = -.044$). One does note that men were far more likely to kill in groups than women, and women far more likely to kill alone than men. This is consistent with the victims: men mortally assaulting each other in gang combats; women secretly murdering their infants. In either figure there appears to be no change over

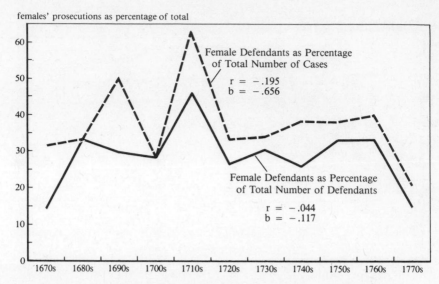

females' prosecutions as percentage of total

Female Defendants as Percentage
of Total Number of Cases

$r = -.195$
$b = -.656$

Female Defendants as Percentage
of Total Number of Defendants

$r = -.044$
$b = -.117$

FIGURE 8. Prosecution of Women for Criminal Homicide as
Percentage of All Prosecutions for Criminal Homicide in
Massachusetts, 1670–1779

time in the ratio of women's criminality. Women simply committed fewer and fewer of the same kinds of homicides; their
rates declined as men's rates declined, but the ratio of their
participation remained undisturbed.

The modern statistics for female homicides—the declining curve of interpersonal violence marking the emergence of
modern society—also confirms only part of the modernization
thesis. As Figure 9 demonstrates, women did increase their
share of homicides in the four decades after 1932. While the
increase is not spectacular, it is steady and strong ($R^2 = .783$).
This makes sense in the light of other criminal arrest statistics
(women are a growing percentage of all types of offenders),
but raises other, prickly questions.[11] The *Uniform Crime Reports*
indicate that women kill alone; their victims are kin or lovers,
and their crime sites are close to home—the same picture that
one obtains from the records of colonial Massachusetts. But if
the crime is the same in its outward shape, why is women's
share of it now increasing?

Let's look at more evidence. In Figure 10 we find an even

arrests of females as percentage of total arrests

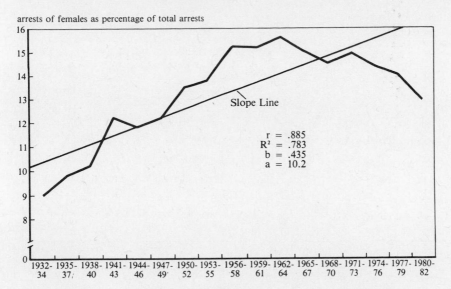

FIGURE 9. Female Arrest for Murder and Non-Negligent Manslaughter, as Percentage of Total Arrests for These Crimes, in the United States, 1932–81

more striking curve in the rate of women's commission of homicide than in their proportion as perpetrators. The bulge between 1965 and 1975 in the rate of women's homicides is strongly correlated with the surge in their ratio of participation in the crime ($r = .654$; $R^2 = .428$). To be sure, men were also committing more homicides in these years, but for a time women outstripped men in the acceleration of their murderous activities. The result is that the pattern of the colonial data—declining rates and stable ratios—has been turned on its side. If the shift in ratio—the increase in women's proportion of all homicides—is partly explained by modernization (that is, more opportunity to commit homicide), how does one explain the rising rate? Can one eat half the cake of modernization and not touch the other half? The strong tie between the two sets of modern figures, the rates and ratios, suggests another, far more complex answer—one that must go beyond the modernization theory.

The rising crime rate for women forces us to consider the limitations of the modernization thesis. While it may describe

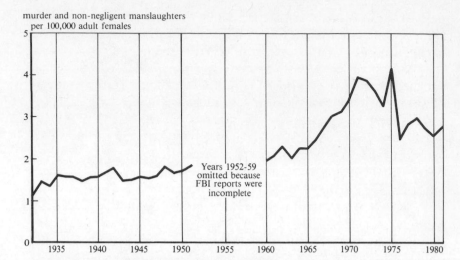

FIGURE 10. Adult Female Murder and Non-Negligent Manslaughter
Rates, in the United States, 1932–81

the increasingly effective controls over behavior in an industrial
society and measure the voluntary acceptance of these controls
by a people in the midst of industrial and technological revolution, it may lose its explanatory power in a postmodern world.
That is, when the social and economic system acts to frustrate
the awakened expectations of hitherto subordinate classes (ethnic minorities, women, and others), they may act out their ag-
gressions against the system against one another. The greatest
leap in women's homicide comes not in times of genuine depression or war, when real hardships were shared, but in times
of progress, when equal opportunity turned out to be more
apparent than real. The timing of the modern surge in offenses
antedates the liberation movement, in effect—figuratively—
making recent women's efforts for political and economic reform into the alternative, the mirror image, of disorganized
acts of criminality by women. When real progress for women
again became possible, when women felt some positive gains
from their organized activity, and when these gains trickled
down to poorer women, the homicide rates dropped dramatically. And when progress stalled, in the early 1980s, the homicide rate—the dark side of protest—once again crept upward.
    The crucial point is this: women's criminal activities are a

part of a continuum from normal to deviant acts, all of which are part of social experience. Women commit crimes, and are prosecuted for crimes, because of their place in a given society. As figures 6–9 demonstrate, the key relationships in that process change over time. The colonial era was stable in terms of sex relationships, but was one of gradually expanding personal freedom for women. Premarital pregnancy rose and official sanctions against such conduct declined in severity. Women's divorce petitions in Massachusetts increased in numbers and were slightly more successful in the courts. The colonial period was one of slowly expanding horizons in culture as well, as urbanization and growing accumulation of wealth gave women greater scope for expression. It was not without foundation that the "Founding Mothers" hoped to share in the political liberties of the Revolution. While the expectations of women advanced, they made relatively few real gains in opportunity for employment or in public life. As the former developments reduced stress, particularly on young mothers, the rate of homicide (primarily the rate of infanticide) declined. Because of the latter, the colonial woman had no more opportunity at the end of the century to commit homicide in the course of other crimes or in public tumults than she had at its start; hence the ratio remained stable and the rate declined.

Twentieth-century America is a different story. Sex roles have been shifting and changing steadily for over forty years, and the increasing and expanding opportunities for women explain, at least in part, the growing ratio of women's homicides. The 1930s witnessed a relaxation of sexual conduct similar to that of the eighteenth century and the later revolution of the 1960s. The early 1930s witnessed an expansion of women's roles both economically and politically. But these decades have also been a period of tremendous stress and frustration for women. The slow progress toward social equality has been a tortuous process that might contribute to the large growth in the per capita increase in female homicide.

Crime—even homicide—is a form of social behavior. As women's social roles open up, so does the possibility for women to engage in crime. This is not to say that feminism is the cause of the growth in female crime, but that increasing female crime is a by-product of more open social opportunities. As we saw with Massachusetts in the colonial period, when social roles stabilize, crime rates level off and stabilize as well (perhaps the tail end of Figure 9 is a sign of better female adjustments to the opportunities—and strains—of modern living).

Historical perspective, in this case our understanding of crime in colonial Massachusetts, has allowed us to see modern crime figures in a different light. It has also taught us that too-general historical theses must often be severely qualified. Perhaps there is more in this lesson. It may be that we are entering a postmodern society, in which the ideals of self-fulfillment and individual realization can no longer be sustained. Minimalist public policy, retrenchment in social services, and rising survivalist sentiment may herald a new and ominous age. If so, it would be a crippling blow to all reform movement and a particularly frustrating one to women. If this is so, the curve of women's violent crime will not stabilize or diminish in the future, but serve, as it has in the past, to witness the anger and frustration of an oppressed group.

I do not wish to close this chapter on the gloomy forecast of a world doomed to postmodern frustration and violence. The highest modern rates of homicide for women and for men do not begin to approach the rates I have found in colonial Massachusetts. Today's woman, for all her thwarted ambitions, turns to violence far less often than her colonial counterpart. Modern social controls work far better in this regard than Puritan ones. If the precision of the foregoing chapters does nothing else, it reassures us of these facts.

NOTES

1. Rita James Simon, *Women and Crime* (Lexington, Mass., 1975), 35 (Table 4.1); data are from the U.S. Department of Justice [Federal Bureau of Investigation], *Uniform Crime Reports* (Washington, D.C., 1932–). This reverses the trend of the previous century, at least in one study: Mary J. Bularziki, "Sex, Crime, and Justice: Women in the Criminal Justice System of Massachusetts" (Ph.D. diss., Brandeis University, 1982), 25 (table).

2. David A. Ward, Maurice Jackson, and Renee E. Ward, "Crimes of Violence by Women," in *Criminology of Deviant Women,* ed. Freda Adler and Rita James Simon (Boston, 1979), 116–17, 120; data from the *Uniform Crime Reports.*

3. Of course, for this and any other study the literature correctly warns that in any full exposition, the size and activity of the law enforcement establishment must also be taken into account.

4. James B. Given, *Society and Homicide in Thirteenth-Century England* (Stanford, 1977), 37, 40, 135. Given's rates of homicide—from a high of 19.8 for Bedfordshire to a low of 6.8 for Kent—have been recalculated to make them rates for *adult* populations. I assumed that about one-half of the population of medieval England was under fourteen.

5. Joel Samaha, *Law and Order in Historical Perspective: The Case of Elizabethan Essex* (New York, 1974), 125–27.

6. Data from William LeHardy, ed., *Calendar to the Middlesex Sessions Records—1613–1618,* new ser., 4 vols. (London, 1935–41).

7. Data from Old Bailey Sessions Papers, 1734–74, Guildhall Library, London, courtesy of Peter C. Hoffer.

8. Simon, *Women and Crime,* 64–65.

9. Peter C. Hoffer and N. E. H. Hull, *Murdering Mothers: Infanticide in England and New England, 1558–1803* (New York, 1981).

10. This most recent survey is Eric H. Monkkonen's "The Organized Response to Crime in Nineteenth–Twentieth-Century America," *Journal of Interdisciplinary History* 14 (Summer 1983), 115–16.

11. Since the 1920s in Great Britain and the 1940s in the United States, crime rates have risen fairly steadily. Ibid., 116.

CONCLUSION

Why study deviant women? For the historian of early America, this is a poignant and pointed question. There can be no question that women were a subordinate class in early American law and society. They were barred from public office, dissuaded from higher education, and exposed to all manner of menial abuse in a world dominated by men. Individuals might rise above the limitations placed upon their sisters, but as a group the highest accolade that women could attain was helpmeet. Is it surprising that some women defied the standards of that society by committing crimes? Hardly—but the evidence presented here points to a very different overall pattern. Women did not resort to crimes to resist their subordination. They committed fewer crimes than men, absolutely, and fewer still measured by their relative numbers. They obeyed the law. They accepted the debilities of being a woman, at least in this respect: if they challenged authority, it was not in the streets. They did not resort to subterfuge or violence to express frustration. They waited and hoped or prepared their children for a better world or fought out their grievances within their homes or suppressed their yearnings or found comfort in religion, good works, and domestic pursuits.

Why did women accept a regime that kept them in partial thrall to others? In part, many may have believed that they were, indeed, inferior creatures in mind and morals. The repayment for this acquiescence was enshrinement in a special place: the good wife who adorned the funeral sermons of Thomas Prince and other ministers. The good wife and mother in this genre of eulogy was the equal of the Puritan man, for her virtues completed his and her graces made home and community viable. Nevertheless, honeyed words at the bier were a poor substitute for equality in life. It was not posthumous literary laurels for the wives of ministers that kept the ordinary New England woman law-abiding—who would believe this of the sweat-soaked, forthright-speaking working women of Boston or Marblehead? They obeyed the law because disobedience brought swift and sanguinary punishment. The criminal law was all around them: in their neighbors' inquisitiveness, the respect they accorded their magistrates, and the status enjoyed by their highest judges. And the repayment to ordinary women for general obedience to the criminal law was far more tangible than any literary reward. The criminal justice system treated women fairly; it did not impose special burdens upon them, nor did it prejudge their guilt.

There were, of course, exceptions to this general rule—the Antinomian Anne Hutchinson, the Quaker Mary Dyer, the witches—which may have involved a special bias against women. These have attracted the attention of scholars, and rightly so, for they are glaring and dramatic examples of the consequences of a prejudicial criminal justice system. All of these incidents, it should be noted, occurred in the seventeenth century. What is more, when one examines the highest courts and the most serious crimes, one finds genuine effort to treat men and women equally, even in that century. True, the law was harsh by modern standards, and moral precepts were even harsher. Defendants had far fewer rights than they do today. But both men and women suffered under these disabilities, in roughly equal proportions. Though the potential for abuse of women in an all-male system of magistrates, jurors, and judges was great, in part because women had no role in the official process of prosecution, that bias did not often manifest itself. Even more important, as this study shows, the modernization of Massachusetts society influenced women's criminality and the treatment of women in the principal courts. Even the blatant prejudice one occasionally finds in the seventeenth-century high courts grew still more uncommon in the eighteenth century. In the end, seeing justice done was a higher calling than acting out prejudices against women.

To the question, "why study deviant women?" the answer is that there is every need to study women as a group, as good wives and as wanton offenders, helpmeets and violators of law, if only to partially exonerate the Puritans and their descendants against the charges of sexism in their laws and courts. And how much the better if that narrower historical end leads us to a fuller appreciation of women's lives in our own day.

A NOTE ON PRIMARY SOURCES

The major primary source for this book was the manuscript court records of the Superior Court of Judicature of Massachusetts, housed in the office of the clerk of the Supreme Judicial Court of Suffolk County, Suffolk County Courthouse, Boston. In room 1402 of that building the thirty-four bound volumes of the Superior Court of the Colony are held, covering the years 1692–1780. The records of special courts of oyer and terminer convened during the tumultuous 1680s are preserved in a separate volume. All of these volumes are roughly chronological, but the volumes overlap and some are half-empty. Each volume of the formal record has a handwritten alphabetical index of cases by litigants. An occasional reference in the index to "indictment" signaled a criminal case, as did the reference "Dominus Rex v." In many cases the table was so incomplete that I had to examine the volumes page by page.

Indictments and proceedings entered in the records were often detailed in describing the defendant and the crime. Still more information was provided by the file papers on the case—coroners' inquests, warrants, depositions, and court orders. These papers are arranged in two chronological series of more than a thousand volumes. Ten volumes of indices—by date, litigants' names, and venue of court—afforded access to the file papers of particular cases.

I have labeled the Superior Court documents "SCJ," followed by the volume and page number of the particular document I am citing. Records of the Superior Court's predecessor, the Court of Assistants, are cited from John Noble et al., eds., *Records of the Court of Assistants of the Colony of Massachusetts Bay, 1629–1692*, 3 vols. (Boston, 1901–28). The relevant statutes are quoted from *Acts and Resolves, Public and Private, of the Province of Massachusetts Bay*, 21 vols. (Boston, 1869–1922), and *The Laws and Liberties of Massachusetts, 1641–1691*, ed. and comp. John D. Cushing, 3 vols. (Wilmington, Del., 1976). English statutes are taken from Danby Pickering et al., comps., *Statutes of the Realm*, (Cambridge, 1762–1832). Other official documents are quoted from *Records of the Governor and Company of Massachusetts Bay*, ed. Nathaniel Shurtleff, 4 vols. (Boston, 1853–64).

APPENDICES

What is the value of a number? Surely numbers—numbers of cases, numbers of imports, price and wage numbers, numbers of votes—are as much the stuff of history as anecdotes and recollections. No one doubts that numbers are evidence. At the same time most historians would agree that quantitative methodology has not swept away more traditional approaches to the study of the past, despite the rhapsodic predictions of a handful of devotees. Quantification has, properly, taken its place beside other relevant special methods, techniques to be used when appropriate to the subject and to the surviving records. The tables and analyses presented in these appendices do not pretend to replace either close examination of particular cases or broad essays on the culture of early modern crime. Instead, they are my attempts to make the fullest use of a magnificently complete and reliable archive. I have tried to suit my methods to the materials, not to overburden their validity with sophisticated statistical trickery. I also am aware that not every historian, and hardly every lay reader, has as much background in statistical argument as the number-crunchers in my own profession. But this book was always intended for educated lay persons, not for the handful of specialists whose work it complements.

Numbers themselves do not say anything. As all historical evidence, they are mute. We give significance to them, as we do to every scrap of surviving record. The numbers here represent forms of official response to allegations of serious crime. It is the patterns of these numbers, their changes over time, their relationships to each other, that should interest the historian. While individual cases might, by some stretch of the historian's imagination be regarded as typical, it is the collective tendency of the data, its trends, that require the most serious attention. Historical facts (and numbers are just that) are relationships, not concrete objects. To ignore the numbers or to fail to bring out all of their interconnections—by artificially isolating one or two cases whose surviving records happen to be especially voluminous, and then microscopically dilating the actions of perpetrators and victims (in actuality constructing long chains of speculation on motive and opportunity)—gives a false concreteness to the past. While the case-study method is illuminating and congenial to popular tastes, it should not exclude examination of the entirety of adjacent criminal records. To ignore other, less well-documented cases on the same docket or of the same type takes the reader away from the historical reality of crime. Thick bundles of affidavits and depositions are seductive, but they only record "what the watchmen saw." The numbers are indispensable.

Appendix 1 is a straightforward compendium of the data discussed in the text. Standard operating procedure in the social sciences requires that collected data be fully displayed, but the conventions of historical style resist tables and charts. I have compromised between the two sets of rules. When the reader must have the full run of data to understand the argument, I have left it in the text. The data not needed to confirm the argument are relegated to this appendix.

Appendix 2 is far more complex and speculative. It is a multiple classification analysis of verdicts. It is too sophisticated for inclusion in the text, where I have summarized the results. The analysis itself comprises the appendices. The explanation should enable the reader to follow my steps. With more data a higher level of reliability could be achieved but, unfortunately, my data set cannot be expanded. It is not a sample, but an entire archive. Thus the conclusions of the MCA are not as striking as they might have been. They were, however, well worth the effort.

Appendix 3 is the beginning of what, I trust, will be a long and mutually enlightening debate with David H. Flaherty on crime in the Bay Colony. The appendix stands on its own; indeed, it might have been an independent publication were it not for the opportunity to present it here. Its conclusions are speculative and will, I hope, become starting points for other scholars' inquiries.

Appendix 1

The Statistics of Crime

These tables display the data used to support the conclusions in Chapter 3. These statistics should not be banished to notes or buried piecemeal in the analysis of crime and punishment. They appear here, collected in appropriate form, following the sequence of analysis in the text.

TABLE A1.1. Marital Status of Women Accused of Serious Crimes, Cross-tabulated by the Type of Crime, SCJ, 1673–1774 (accompanies page 55 of text)

		Marital Status			
		Single	Married	Widowed	Row Total
	Homicide	54 (72.0%)	18 (24.0%)	3 (4.0%)	75 [37.3%]
	Other Personal	18 (40.9%)	19 (43.2%)	7 (15.9%)	44 [21.9%]
Serious Crime	Sophisticated Property	4 (40.0%)	3 (30.0%)	3 (30.0%)	10 [5.0]
	Other Property	23 (57.5%)	15 (37.5%)	2 (5.0%)	40 [19.9%]
	Sexual Morals	6 (18.8%)	26 (81.2%)	0 (0%)	32 [15.9%]
	Column Total	105 (52.2%)	81 (40.3%)	15 (7.5%)	201 [(100%)]

Note. ( ) = row percentages; [ ] = column percentages.

TABLE A1.2. Residence of Women Accused of Serious Crimes, 1673–1774
(accompanies page 57 of text)

Residence	Number of Cases	Percentage of Total
Same city and county as trial	71	31.7
Same county, but different city or rural	105	46.9
Recently moved to county	1	0.4
Different county	11	4.9
Unknown	36	16.1
Total	224	100.0

TABLE A1.3. Ethnic/Racial Identity of Women Accused of Serious Crimes
(using names and other identifying notes in the record), 1673–1774
(accompanies page 57 of text)

Ethnic/Racial Background	Number of Cases	Percentage of Total
English	188	83.9
Irish	3	1.3
Scots	1	0.4
German	2	0.9
Black	16	7.1
Mulatto	2	0.9
Indian	12	5.4
Total	224	100.0

TABLE A1.4. Racial Identity of Women Accused of Serious Crimes,
Cross-tabulated by the Type of Crime, 1673–1774
(accompanies page 58 of text)

| | | Racial Identity | | | |
		White	Black	Indian	Row Total
	Homicide	56 (72.7%) [29.2%]	12 (15.6%) [66.6%]	9 (11.7%) [75%]	77 [34.7%] (100%)
	Other Personal	47 (95.9%) [24.5%]	2 (4.1%) [11.1%]	0	49 [22.1%] (100%)
Serious Crime	Sophisticated Property	11 (100%) [5.7%]	0	0	11 [5.0%] (100%)
	Other Property	43 (86%) [22.4%]	4 (8%) [22.2%]	3 (6%) [25%]	50 [22.5%] (100%)
	Sexual/Morality	35 (100%) [18.2%]	0	0	35 [15.8%] (100%)
	Column Total	192 (86.5%) [100%]	18 (8.1%) [100%]	12 (5.4%) [100%]	

Note. ( ) = row percentages; [ ] = column percentages.

TABLE A1.5 Ages of Victims of Serious Crimes Attributed to Women,
1673–1774 (accompanies page 59 of text)

Age	Number of Cases	Percentage of Total
Neonate (one day old)	44	29.9
Under 2 years	10	6.8
2–8 years	3	2.0
Child unspecified	10	6.8
Adult	80	54.4
Total	147	100.0

Appendix 1

TABLE A1.6. Relationship of Victims to Women Accused of Serious Crimes, 1673–1774 (accompanies page 59 in text)

Relationship	Number of Cases	Percentage of Total
Spouse	1	0.6
Child (son/daughter)	62	37.6
Master	6	3.6
Related but Unspecified	3	1.8
None	93	56.4
Total	165	100.0

TABLE A1.7. Gender of Victims of Women Accused of Serious Crimes, Cross-tabulated by the Type of Crime, 1673–1774 (accompanies page 60 in text)

		Gender of Victim		
		Female	Male	Row Total
Serious	Homicide	24 (44.4%) [36.9%]	30 (55.6%) [41.7%]	54 [39.4]
Crime	Other Personal	28 (75.7%) [43.1%]	9 (24.3%) [12.5%]	37 [27.0%]
	Property	13 (28.3%) [20.0%]	33 (71.7%) [45.8%]	46 [33.6%]
	Column Total	65 (47.4%)	72 (52.6%)	137

Note. ( ) = row percentages; [ ] = column percentages.

Appendix 2
Multiple Classification Analysis of Verdicts

Table A2.1 is a multiple classification analysis (MCA) of female conviction by four independent variables: the marital status of the accused, the ethnicity/race of the accused, the classification of the offense as capital or non-capital, and the type of crime (personal, property, sophisticated property, sex and morals, or public).

The "Grand Mean" is the percentage of convictions for women rounded to hundredths.[1] Column "N" is the number of cases for which information was available on the variable to the left. The "unadjusted deviation" is the effect that each category of the variables had upon the verdict. For example, "single" (category 1 of the variable "marital") led to a five-percentage-point increase in conviction rate, whereas being "married" decreased the likelihood of conviction by six percentage points. "Eta" is a statistical measure of the strength of association between any variable and the verdict—the extent to which the two co-varied. In this case, marital status was not strongly related to verdicts, co-varying with verdicts only 14 percent of the time. This fits our earlier cross-tabulation. The unadjusted deviation does not control for the effects the other three variables—ethnicity/race of suspects, severity of crime, and type of crime—might have had upon the way that the jury conceived the marital status of the accused. For example, if the jury saw that the accused was black, it might take a very different view of the accused's marital status. Among these unadjusted variables, only the severity of the crime seems to have had a strong association with verdicts (eta = .34).

One conclusion stands out: if a crime was capital, juries were more lenient—in fact, twelve percentage points beneath the overall conviction rate. In non-capital crimes, the jury was more severe, twenty-two points above the mean conviction rate. So many of women's crimes were capital in the high courts, however, that the severity of verdicts was more often muted than exacerbated. As has already been demonstrated, the race of the non-white accused had a

TABLE A2.1. Multiple Classification Analysis of Female Conviction
by Marital Status, Ethnicity/Race of the Accused, Severity of the Offense,
and Type of Crime

Grand Mean = 0.38 Variable + Category	N	Unadjusted Deviation	ETA	Deviation Adjusted for Other Independent Variables	BETA
Marital Status					
Unknown	20	−0.03		−0.10	
Single	105	0.05		0.08	
Married	81	−0.06		−0.10	
Widowed	15	−0.05		0.03	
Separated	1	0.62		0.78	
			0.14		0.21
Ethnicity/Race					
White	192	−0.01		−0.01	
Black	18	0.29		0.27	
Indian	12	−0.30		−0.20	
			0.22		0.19
Capital Offense?					
Yes	142	−0.12		−0.13	
No	80	0.22		0.23	
			0.34		0.36
Type of Crime					
Homicide	77	−0.09		−0.02	
Other personal	49	−0.13		−0.08	
Sophisticated property	11	−0.01		−0.24	
Other property	50	0.22		0.10	
Sex and morals	35	0.08		0.08	
			0.28		0.18

Multiple R^2: 0.229
Multiple R: 0.478

Note. 222 cases were tabulated; the table is significant at the 10 percent level.

major effect upon the verdict: blacks were convicted twenty-nine
percentage points more often than the average, and Indians thirty
percentage points less often. So many defendants were white that
the overall relationship between conviction and race remains weak.

A comparison of each of these four variables with conviction rates, with the other three variables held constant (as if the jury did not know the other information), produces the "adjusted deviation." If the jury did not know anything about the defendant other than marital status, her "single" status added three additional percentage points to the conviction rate (from an unadjusted deviation of .05, hence a 43 percent conviction rate, to an adjusted deviation of .08, hence a conviction rate of 46 percent). Conversely, if the jury knew only that the defendant was married, her conviction rate went down four percentage points (from an adjusted deviation of −.06, a 32 percent conviction rate, to an adjusted deviation of −.10, a 28 percent conviction rate). At the same time, the strength of the relationship between marital status and conviction rate—in other words, the impact that knowledge of marital status would have on the deliberations of the jury in the absence of additional information—increases from .14 to .21 (the "beta" is another measure of covariation). This is not a great increase, but it does show that additional information tended to blur the jurors' slightly negative attitude toward spinsters. This increase in effect and association did not appear in the ethnicity/race of the accused or the severity of the crime: each had the same effect upon jurors and correlated similarly with convictions, whether or not the jurors knew more about the defendants than their race or whether their offense was capital. The type of crime actually decreased in its association with verdicts when all other variables were held constant (beta was .18, while eta was .28). This is again not a large decline nor are the figures significant, but the decrease in impact of type of crime upon the jurors when it was isolated from the simultaneous effects of other information shows that the type of crime was viewed in the context of the rest of the information. In other words, the type of crime was less important to the jurors than the interconnection among the type of crime, the marital status and ethnicity/race of the accused, and the nature of the crime.

The multiple R squared at the bottom of the table is the total explanatory power of all the independent variables upon the conviction rate. Here, it means that these four kinds of information explained about one-quarter of the variation in the conviction rate. The multiple R, a measure of correlation, was nearly .5, fairly high for any empirical historical study. Other MCA programs showed smaller R and R^2 statistics, as would be expected, since the variables in Table A2.1 were the strongest indicators when taken singly or in cross-tabulations.

To bring the effect of gender into a MCA, Table A1.2 was prepared for all male and female defendants accused of capital offenses. Again, I chose to limit it to capital offenses to avoid basing male and female conviction rates upon different kinds of crimes.

TABLE A2.2. Multiple Classification Analysis of Capital Conviction by Sex of the Accused, Type of Crime, and Decade of Occurrence

Grand Mean = 0.36 Variable + Category	N	Unadjusted Deviation	ETA	Deviation Adjusted for Other Independent Variables	BETA
Sex of the Accused					
Female	130	−0.12		−0.14	
Male	221	0.07		0.08	
			0.18		0.23
Type of Crime					
Homicide	232	0.03		0.03	
Other personal	53	−0.08		−0.09	
Other property	34	−0.10		−0.07	
Sex and morals	19	−0.05		0.07	
Public	13	0.18		0.00	
			0.12		0.10
Decade					
1670s	44	0.00		−0.02	
1680s	23	0.12		0.17	
1690s	64	0.04		0.14	
1700s	19	0.25		0.20	
1710s	22	−0.13		−0.14	
1720s	47	−0.19		−0.22	
1730s	22	0.00		−0.06	
1740s	21	0.07		0.08	
1750s	31	0.06		0.04	
1760s	28	−0.08		−0.09	
1770s	31	0.03		−0.04	
			0.22		0.27

Multiple R^2: 0.106
Multiple R: 0.325

Note. 353 cases were processed; the table is significant at the 10 percent level.

Male non-capital offenses were different from female non-capital offenses, and adding such dissimilar types of offenses into an analysis of the effect of gender upon verdicts would lead to conclusions based upon two very different data bases.

The multiple R^2 of this table is not great, only .106, which means that the variables in it do not explain much of the pattern of convictions in the Superior Court of Judicature. The table does show that when other variables are controlled, the sex of the accused had a slightly larger impact on the deliberations of jurors. The percentage of conviction also declines very slightly for women (and increases very slightly for men) when adjusted for the type of crime and the decade in which it was committed. The type of crime had little effect on the jurors, and, again, when separated from other information about the criminal, the crime actually declined in importance in helping jurors to reach a verdict. The effect of time expends its effect through an intervening variable—the type of crime. A number of other variables were inserted into other MCAs, with similar results. Explanations of the conviction of women are more plausibly sought within the characteristics of women's lives and the details of their crimes than in comparisons with the men's situations.

NOTE

1. I have turned conviction, a categorical variable, into an interval level variable by creating the fiction that the severity of the verdict was numerical and assigning an 0 to an acquittal and a 1 to a conviction. On multiple classification analysis, see Jae-On Kim and Frank J. Kohout, "Analysis of Variance and Covariance," in *Statistical Package for the Social Sciences,* ed. Norman H. Nie et al., rev. 2d ed. (New York, 1975), 400–422, and Richard Jensen, "New Presses for Old Grapes I: Multiple Classification Analysis," *Historical Methods* 11 (Fall 1978), 174.

Appendix 3

The External Causes of Crime in Massachusetts, 1700–1774

In his recent essay on crime in eighteenth-century Massachusetts, David H. Flaherty challenged other scholars to delineate the relationship between hardship and crimes against property. He is absolutely right when he claims that "it is unusual to find direct evidence that actual economic need inspired a particular criminal act." His own investigation of the 1720s, a decade of fluctuating economic conditions in Massachusetts, did not show either dramatic or certain ties between hardship and crimes against property. Of course, in the light of the relatively low rate of crimes against property in the colony generally, such shifts in decadal rates could easily be swallowed by larger trends.[1] Indeed, as Chapter 3 indicated, the century was marked by a steadily declining rate of all types of crimes.

Would a more rigorous investigation of "external" factors show stronger ties between palpable needs and measurable criminality? Let us see. Figure A3.1 plots the totals of thefts-by-trick (for example, counterfeiting) and thefts-by-force (for example, robbery and larceny) for every year from 1680 through 1774. The data are taken from the records of the Courts of Assistants and Superior Court of Judicature.

The first and simplest way of relating these crimes to external events is to plot the yearly numbers of each type of crime, and when yearly crimes are compared to external events there are some obvious correlations. External events in individual years suggest explanations for several sudden shifts in number and type of serious property crimes. The sudden jump in thefts-by-trick in 1750 (point A on the graph) can be connected to the switchover in that year from paper money to specie: currency violators tried to cash in altered or counterfeited bills (in addition, finance-conscious authorities pursued potential defrauders with extra diligence). The dearth of property crimes during this period of specie change in 1752 (point B) can be attributed to the smallpox epidemic that devastated Boston in

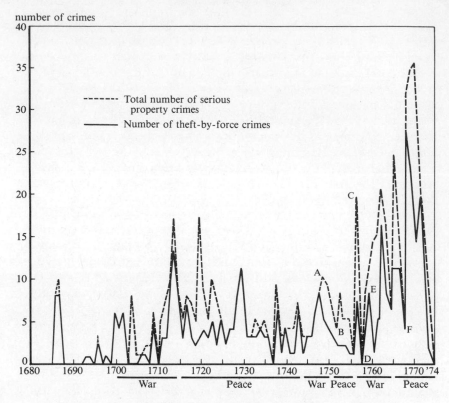

number of crimes

FIGURE A3.1. Absolute Number of Serious Property Crimes in
Massachusetts, by Year, 1680–1774

that year.[2] Economic activity nearly halted as thousands died and
thousands more evacuated the city—including government officials.
Opportunity to defraud simply dried up during the crisis. Currency
violators increased activity again in 1757 (point C), as Boston sought
to finance its disastrous debt. A boom in sophisticated property
crimes—fraud and counterfeiting—occurred early in the French
and Indian wars. This was immediately followed by a trough in
which no one was charged with any serious property crimes (point
D). The beginning of hostilities required funding of military expedi-
tions and provided opportunities for thefts-by-trick. Yet as war progressed—particularly in 1758, the height of wartime military activity, when the Fortress of Louisburg was taken by English and colonial troops for a second time—men and women were occupied and
generally uninvolved in or unconcerned with property crimes. In
addition, the colony was probably drained of able-bodied men, those

most likely to commit theft-by-force crimes and initiate theft-by-trick crimes. No events were as pervasively influential in the provincial years as the periods of war and peace. When crime rates (the number of crimes in a period of time divided by the number of people at risk to commit them) for periods of peace are compared with crime rates for periods of war, there is no overall pattern; war did not incite or depress serious property crimes. However, looking back at the yearly graph of crimes, one finds that in the years immediately after the end of hostilities, there were sudden jumps in theft-by-force crimes. Some young men coming home from battle took to crime—crimes of force are associated with that age group. This phenomenon occurred in 1713–14, 1748–49, and 1761–63.

The 1760s and early 1770s saw an increase of serious property crimes. In these years the Massachusetts economy, particularly in Boston, experienced increasingly hard times. The number of serious property crimes was a response, perhaps, to the depression. The one exceptional year, 1768 (point F), in which both types of crime declined dramatically, was the year British troops arrived in Boston, temporarily intimidating those inclined toward committing property crimes. One last observation must be made: in those years in which Massachusetts civil-political disruptions were greatest—1765 (the Stamp Act riots) and 1770 (the Boston Massacre)—criminal activity dropped sharply. Either the populace was directing its energy toward mob violence rather than criminal strife, or authorities were too preoccupied by the former to pay much attention to the latter. This phenomenon, by either explanation, tends to support the Enrico Ferri thesis, later applied to New England by Kai T. Erikson, that society needs or tolerates a fairly stable level of deviance and compensates in one area for exceptional swings in another.[3]

Do more general external factors significantly influence serious crimes against property? One major preoccupation of modern criminology—the urban roots of crime—is easily applied to our data. Did serious property crime rates in Boston exceed those outside of the city? If so, why? Figure A3.2 illustrates the number and type of serious property crimes committed in Boston and the rest of the colony. Theft-by-trick was slightly more prevalent in the countryside outside Boston—areas bordering other colonies perhaps provided greater opportunity for illegal maneuvers with neighboring currencies. Swings in the number and type of crime over time, however, are very similar for the two geographic areas.

While the types of serious crimes against property in urban and rural areas were similar, the absolute numbers do not reflect the proportion of crimes committed in the city and the countryside over

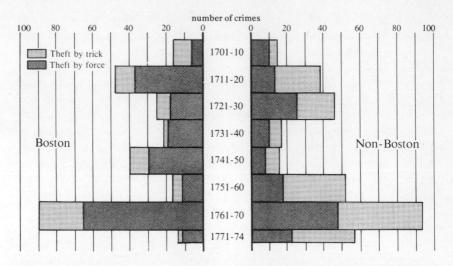

FIGURE A3.2. Serious Property Crimes, Boston and Non-Boston, by Decade, 1701–74

time. The population of Boston was never more than a fraction of that of the rest of the colony and that fraction apparently declined over the course of the eighteenth century. Nevertheless, as Figure A3.3 shows, decadal crime rates for all serious property crimes in Boston were always the highest. Three important conclusions can be drawn from the data presented in this figure.

First, fluctuations in Boston and non-Boston crime rates are not very highly correlated ($r = .498$), that is, they do not vary together. External conditions either did not affect the city and countryside similarly (a reasonable possibility since, for example, if wheat prices increased it would mean higher incomes for farmers but lower net incomes for cityfolk paying higher prices for bread) or internal conditions in dissimilar geographic areas were more important to patterns of crime. Both of these suggestions are explored below. Second, Boston and non-Boston crime rates are not reciprocal, that is, it would not appear that criminals left one geographic area to commit crimes in the other. Third, and most important, the crime rate for Boston is significantly higher than for non-Boston. This fact is explicit in the difference in rates in numerical terms. See Table A3.1.

Even a cursory glance at these figures indicates that Boston's serious property crime rate is near or exceeds ten times the non-Boston rate in seven of the eight decades. High rates of crime seem to be an urban phenomenon. All three observations reinforce the

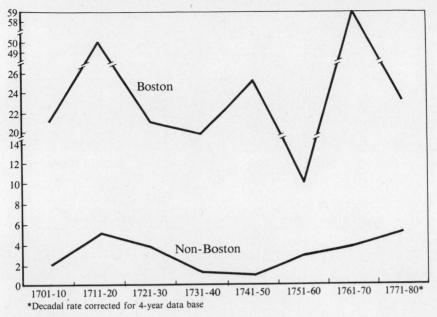

FIGURE A3.3. Serious Property Crime Rates, Boston and Non-Boston, by Decade* per 10,000 Population, 1701–80

notion that rural and city crime are two distinct phenomena, with city crime dominating the two.

This result is consistent with contemporary criminological theory. Can the phenomenon then be explained by modern hypotheses on the origins of urban crime? Density of population is a defining characteristic of cities and has been offered as an explanation of some types of property crimes. Does changing density correlate with changing rates of crime in eighteenth-century Boston? The geographical boundaries of Boston changed little during this time. The crime rate in Table A3.1 can be regressed with decadal population shifts in the city to determine whether the two are related. A dismal $r = -.145$ indicates that no real relationship exists between crime and density of population.

Since urban herding is not in itself the answer to the question of higher urban crime rates, perhaps a subtler mechanism is at work. Cities are centers of mercantile activity. Consumer goods and personal wealth are visible and concentrated in marketplaces and private homes, providing opportunity and incentive for economic crimes. Using Gary B. Nash's figures on distribution of wealth among Boston testators, I calculated the difference between the rich-

TABLE A3.1. Boston and Non-Boston Serious Property Crime Rates, by Decade

	Boston	Non-Boston
Years	Rate per 10,000 population (N)	Rate per 10,000 population (N)
1701–10	21.33 (16)	2.22 (15)
1711–20	49.85 (49)	5.12 (39)
1721–30	21.12 (25)	3.83 (37)
1731–40	13.88 (22)	1.35 (17)
1741–50	25.25 (41)	1.05 (16)
1751–60	9.58 (15)	2.71 (52)
1761–70	58.63 (91)	4.05 (95)
1771–74	22.51[a] (14)	5.36[a] (58)

[a]This is a decadal rate corrected for the four-year data base.

est and poorest groups of decedants and used the difference as an indicator of the relative distribution of wealth in the city.[4] When the distribution of wealth is regressed with Boston's rate of serious property offenses for the six decades prior to the Revolution—1716–74—one obtains quite a striking correlation ($r = .890$; $R^2 = .793$). The association between the distribution of wealth in society and its crime rate is powerful—and makes good sense.

Density alone does not explain high urban crime rates, but the offshoot of density—widespread awareness of the growing gap between the rich and the poor (a slope of 37.11)—does explain the course of serious property crime. Alice Hanson Jones has recently remarked that "urban wealth was plainly visible in such cities [as colonial Boston].... There also were urban poor in all these cities.... Data from other studies suggest that wealth inequality was greater in large cities than in rural areas."[5] The gap between rich

Table A3.2. Difference in Median Wealth between the Richest and Poorest
Testators in Boston, 1716–74, vs. Serious Property Crime Rate

Period	Serious Property Crime Rate per 10,000 Population	Difference in Wealth, Poorest vs. Wealthiest (£)[a]
1716–25	29.61	1269
1726–35	17.59	1091
1736–45	14.94	1053
1746–55	21.31	1441
1756–65	32.71	1539
1766–74[b]	41.21	2192

Note. Regression statistics: $r = .890$; $R^2 = .793$; slope $= 37.11$.

[a]Data are derived from Gary B. Nash, *The Urban Crucible: Social Change, Political Consciousness, and the Origins of the American Revolution* (Cambridge, Mass., 1979), 400.

[b]Rate and difference in wealth have been corrected for the nine-year period.

and poor widened particularly rapidly in the economically troubled decades of the 1750s, 1760s, and 1770s; the number of property crimes took off concurrently.

The obvious importance of the urban setting in explaining the shifts in property crimes rates and the availability of economic data on Boston allow us to probe the relationship between deprivation and crime more deeply. We have discovered that the distribution of wealth, so visibly disparate in the city, does have a strong relationship to property crime rates. Indicators of external economic conditions for the poorer half of society—the extent of dire poverty, the price of basic commodities, and the economic health of the port of Boston—have a far weaker association with crime rates. Nash has calculated the average yearly poor relief rate by decade for eighteenth-century Boston.[6] There is a very small correlation between the amount of poor relief and the rate of property crimes by decade ($r = .392$), and this does not really explain the change in serious property crimes over time ($R^2 = .154$). Poor relief is not an ideal direct indicator, however, since it is based on the largesse of the authorities, a quixotic inclination that could vary over time from many other considerations besides need. The classic economic indicator is the price of wheat, a commodity basic to all levels of society and one for which we have yearly figures.[7] I did four regressions of yearly wheat prices with the number of crimes in Boston. First, I divided the period 1730–74 into two periods, to compensate for the switch in price quotations from paper money to specie after 1749. Second, I tried a direct regression as well as a one-year lag regression. The one-year lag regression allowed for the effect of the change in wheat prices to filter down through the economy. The direct regression double checks the possibility that change in prices had an immediate effect on the ordinary citizen. All regressions were between the absolute number of crimes and the first differences in wheat prices. First differences focus on direction and magnitude of change rather than absolute price—intuitively a better indicator. For 1730–49, both regressions (direct and one-year lag) are very weak ($r = .229$ and $+.257$, respectively). For 1751–74, the one-year lag regression was even weaker ($r = .133$), but the direct regression was modest ($r = -.420$). Changing wheat prices had almost no relation and certainly no causative effect upon property crime rates, at least for serious crimes.

A last indicator of economic conditions for the poor was the balance of trade.[8] Boston was dependent upon its port for much of its wealth. In Table A3.3, I compare and then regress first differences in the mean five-year balance of trade between England and

TABLE A3.3. Serious Property Crimes and First Differences in Mean Five-Year Balance of Trade between England and New England, 1730–74

| Period | Mean Balance (1000 £) | First Difference | Number of Serious Property Crimes | | |
			Boston	Non-Boston	Mass.
1726–30	−127.2	—	14	15	29
1731–35	−122.04	5.16	10	10	20
1736–40	−146.54	−24.5	12	7	19
1741–45	−107.68	38.86	12	9	21
1746–50	−200.20	−92.52	29	7	36
1751–55	−249.80	−46.6	5	23	28
1756–60	−434.20	−184.4	10	29	39
1761–65	−271.00	163.2	41	33	74
1766–70	−228.32	42.68	50	62	112
1771–74[a]	−705.00	−476.68	14	58	72

Note. Boston: $r = .405$; $R^2 = .164$; slope = .035
   non-Boston: $r = -.040$; $R^2 = .002$; slope = −.007
   Massachusetts: $r = -.361$; $R^2 = .130$; slope = −.042.
[a]Data are corrected for the four-year period.

New England ports against the five-year serious property crime totals for Boston, the provinces, and all of Massachusetts. These regression statistics are weak, suggesting no strong link between imbalance of trade and property crimes.

It is possible that the combined effect of these three indicators
of economic conditions may be far stronger an influence upon palpable need than anyone of them alone: if they are truly independent
variables, their influences may be additive. Their combined effect
upon variation in the number of prosecutions for serious crimes
against property in Boston can be calculated with multiple regression techniques. A multiple regression of relief levels, changes in
wheat prices, and first differences in the balance of trade upon the
rate of serious crimes against property in Boston reveals a combined
covariance (R^2) of less than 30 percent, however. Even Boston reveals a combined covariance (R^2) of less than 30 percent. Even when
hardship was all around, crime among the needy classes did not
increase very much. They, as the women we have studied, generally
obeyed the law.

I fear that I have not given David Flaherty the definitive answer
that he desired, but, in apology, I cite the same fact that he found
compelling. Between the commission of the crime and the prosecution of the accused lies a complex set of decisions, and not all of
these, by any means, were made by those in authority. External
forces clearly had some effect upon the commission of the crime, but
precise measurement of these effects is very difficult. The conditions
under which the motive to commit a crime outweighed the deterrent
effect of magisterial displeasure and community resistance clearly
varied in individual cases.

NOTES

1. David H. Flaherty, "Crime and Social Control in Provincial Massachusetts," *Historical Journal* 24 (1981), 352–55.

2. Carl Bridenbaugh, *Cities in Revolt: Urban Life in America, 1743–
1776* (New York, 1955), 7, 18, 48, 61, 129, 298.

3. Kai T. Erikson, *Wayward Puritans: A Study in the Sociology of Deviance* (New York, 1966), ch. 4.

4. The median differences are derived from figures in Gary B. Nash,
*The Urban Crucible: Social Change, Political Consciousness, and the Origins of the
American Revolution* (Cambridge, Mass., 1979), 400. The figures include real
estate.

5. Alice Hanson Jones, *Wealth of a Nation to Be: The American Colonies
on the Eve of the Revolution* (New York, 1980), 321.

6. Nash, *Urban Crucible,* 402.

7. The first differences of the wheat prices are derived from data in Arthur H. Cole, *Wholesale Commodity Prices in the United States, 1700–1861* (Cambridge, Mass., 1938), 117.

8. First differences of mean balance of trade are derived from data given in Bureau of the Census, *Historical Statistics of the United States, Colonial Times to 1970,* Part II (Washington, D. C., 1975), 1176–77.

INDEX

Adams, Abigail: and women's roles, 15

Adams, John: counsel for Elizabeth Eams, 98

Adultery, 44, 46; defined, 29–30; as women's crimes, 29–30, 32, 53–54; punishment for, 31; penalties reduced, 34; and racial minorities, 58

American Revolution: change in women's roles as result of, 15; expectation of women after, 137

Andrews, Susannah: indicted for infanticide, 97; executed, 115

Anna: given 60 stripes, 113

Appeal, 82

Arson, 44, 51; defined, 19, 24, 51; punishment in Massachusetts, 34; and minorities, 58

Ashley, Meriam: indicted for counterfeiting, 82

Assault, 44, 46, 51; and gender, 62

Baldwin, Moses, 124

Bartlett, Sarah: accused of arson, 80

Bastardy: and poor laws, 25; and infanticide, 26, 47; and gender of accused, 32; punishment of, 66

Benefit of clergy, 34–36, 115; and punishment, 114

Bestiality, 26, 34

Bettee: convicted of infanticide, 96

Bias: against women, 9, 21, 24; against minorities, 9, 57, 101–2, 104–5; in felony law, 21, 24, 106; in criminal proceedings, 73–74, 84, 88–89, 94–95, 99–100; among jurors, 99–100, 106–7; in sentencing, 116–18; in criminal justice system, 141. *See also* Deviance

Bigamy, 114

Black, Charles, Jr.: on bias, 94

Blacks: and crime, 51, 57; and verdicts, 106; and punishment, 116–17, 119–20

Blackstone, William: defines felony, 22, 23, 24; on defendant's rights, 90

Blasphemy, 29

Body of Liberties (1648), 29

Bosco, Robert: discussion of execution sermons, 124

Branding (as punishment). *See* Mutilation

Burglary, 44; defined, 19, 24, 32, 34; and gender, 62

Callegharne, Margaret: charged with infanticide, 74–75

Capital punishment: and felony law, 22–23, 37–38n21; in Massachusetts codes, 29; impact on verdicts, 105; impact on sentencing, 109, 117; and women, 110, 115–16

Center, Sarah: charged with assault, 52, 95

Chamblit, Rebecca: indicted for infanticide, 77–78

Chaplin, Margaret: tried for passing counterfeit currency, 82

Chauncy, Charles, 124

Children: declining mortality rates of, 16; and arson, 51. *See also* Infanticide

Clark, Mary: charged with theft, 35

Clefson, Eunice: convicted of incest, 114

Codes (criminal): in Massachusetts, 28–29, 31; and gender-specific offenses, 29, 34; and felony, 40n54

A Note on the Author

N. E. H. Hull received her Ph.D. in history from Columbia University in 1981 and her J.D. from the University of Georgia in 1985. She is the co-author (with Peter Charles Hoffer) of two books, *Murdering Mothers: Infanticide in England and New England, 1558–1805,* and *Impeachment in America, 1635–1805.* She is presently a resident fellow at Harvard University's Charles Warren Center for Studies in American History and is working on a new book, *The New Jurisconsults: The American Law Institute and the Transformation of American Law in the Twentieth Century.* Dr. Hull is also a member of the Georgia bar.